P9-CBK-413

Modern Critical Interpretations

Adventures of Huckleberry Finn
All Quiet on the Western Front
Animal Farm
Beloved
Beowulf
Billy Budd, Benito Cereno, Bartleby the
    Scrivener, and Other Tales
The Bluest Eye
The Catcher in the Rye
Catch-22
Cat on a Hot Tin Roof
Cat's Cradle
The Color Purple
Crime and Punishment
The Crucible
Daisy Miller, The Turn of the Screw,
    and Other Tales
David Copperfield
Death of a Salesman
The Divine Comedy
Don Quixote
Dubliners
Emma
Fahrenheit 451
A Farewell to Arms
Frankenstein
The General Prologue to the
    Canterbury Tales
The Glass Menagerie
The Grapes of Wrath
Great Expectations
The Great Gatsby
Gulliver's Travels
Hamlet
The Handmaid's Tale
Heart of Darkness
The Joy Luck Club
The Jungle
I Know Why the Caged Bird Sings
The Iliad
The Interpretation of Dreams
Invisible Man
Jane Eyre
Julius Caesar
King Lear
Long Day's Journey into Night
Lord Jim
Lord of the Flies

The Lord of the Rings
Macbeth
The Merchant of Venice
The Metamorphosis
A Midsummer Night's Dream
Moby-Dick
My Ántonia
Native Son
Night
1984
The Odyssey
Oedipus Rex
One Flew Over the Cuckoo's Nest
The Old Man and the Sea
Othello
Paradise Lost
The Pardoner's Tale
A Portrait of the Artist as a Young Man
Pride and Prejudice
Ragtime
The Red Badge of Courage
The Rime of the Ancient Mariner
Romeo and Juliet
The Scarlet Letter
A Scholarly Look at the Diary of
    Anne Frank
A Separate Peace
Slaughterhouse Five
Song of Solomon
The Sonnets
Sophie's Choice
The Sound and the Fury
The Stranger
A Streetcar Named Desire
Sula
The Sun Also Rises
A Tale of Two Cities
The Tales of Poe
The Tempest
Tess of the D'Urbervilles
Their Eyes Were Watching God
Things Fall Apart
To Kill a Mockingbird
Ulysses
Waiting for Godot
Walden
The Waste Land
Wuthering Heights

Modern Critical Interpretations

Upton Sinclair's
The Jungle

Edited and with an introduction by
Harold Bloom
Sterling Professor of the Humanities
Yale University

CHELSEA HOUSE PUBLISHERS
Philadelphia

Library of Congress Cataloging-in-Publication Data

Upton Sinclair's The Jungle / edited and with an introduction by
Harold Bloom.

      p. cm.—(Modern critical interpretations)
    Includes bibliographical references and index.
    ISBN 0-7910-6341-0 (alk. paper)
    1. Sinclair, Upton, 1878–1968. Jungle. 2. Political fiction,
America—History and criticism. 3. Chicago (Ill.—In literature.
4. Working class in literature. 5. Immigrants in literature.
I. Bloom, Harold. II. Series.

PS3537 .I85 J973 2001
813'.52—dc21   2001047152

Chelsea House Publishers
1974 Sproul Road, Suite 400
Broomall, PA 19008-0914

The Chelsea House World Wide Web address is
http://www.chelseahouse.com

Series Editor: Matt Uhler

Contributing Editor: Pamela Loos

Produced by Publisher's Services, Santa Barbara, California

Contents

Editor's Note

My Introduction reluctantly admits that *The Jungle* (1906) is a period piece: to read it, one puts one's uphill shoulder to the wheel, and feels proper gratitude to Upton Sinclair's book, which helped give us the Pure Food and Drug Act of 1906.

Jon A. Yoder sadly comments that the public received *The Jungle* as muckraking, rather than as an indictment of capitalism, while Michael Brewster Folsom accurately indicts Upton Sinclair for racism, and for spoiling his novel's conclusion.

A poignant defense of the book is offered by the scholarly and brilliant Morris Dickstein, who tries to save *The Jungle* by citing our New Age of the nonfiction novel and the New Journalism, after which Timothy Cook usefully traces the influence of Upton Sinclair's novel upon George Orwell's *Animal Farm*.

In R. N. Mookerjee's reading, the novel comes apart when Sinclair moves from a vision of human suffering to a sermon for socialism, while Emory Elliott, though acknowledging Sinclair's racism, praised him for showing the destructive effect upon poor people when they live without hope for the future.

The analogue between Jack London's *The Call of the Wild* and *The Jungle* is worked through by Jacqueline Tavernier-Courbin, after which Scott Derrick meditates upon Sinclair's bondage to masculine myths of gender-rules.

In this volume's final essay, Matthew J. Morris interestingly analyzes Sinclair's unsuccessful struggle to find a narrative mode that could show the killing power of capitalism without adding just one more representation of that power that involuntarily helps to prolong it.

Introduction

In his ninety years Upton Sinclair wrote ninety books, almost got elected Governor of California (1934), and died knowing that he had helped pass the Pure Food and Drug Act of 1906, and had lived to be Lyndon Johnson's guest observer of the signing of the Wholesome Meat Act (1967). That is hardly a wasted life, though *The Jungle* is now only a rather drab period piece, and the other books are totally unreadable.

Morris Dickstein and Emory Elliott between them have done as much as can be done for *The Jungle*, which I have just reread, with curiosity and revulsion, more than half-a-century after my first encounter with the book. I dimly recall having found it both somber and harrowing, but I was very young, and both experiential and literary sorrows have made me more impatient with it now. American naturalistic writing can survive a certain crudity in style and procedure; Dreiser in particular transcends such limitations in *Sister Carrie* and *An American Tragedy*. But Sinclair has nothing of Dreiser's preternatural powers of empathy. What Sinclair tries to do is simply beyond his gifts: his people are names on the page, and his inability to represent social reality makes me long for Balzac and Zola, or even Tom Wolfe.

Time is cruel to inadequate literature, though it can be slow in its remorselessness. The young have a remarkable taste for period pieces; I note that my paperback copy of *The Jungle*, published in 1981, is in its thirty-third printing, and I suspect that most of it has been sold to younger people, in or out of class. I meditate incessantly on the phenomenon of period pieces, surrounded as I am by so many bad books proclaimed as instant classics, while John Crowley's *Little, Big* (1981), a fantasy novel I have read through scores of times, is usually out-of-print, as it is at the moment. Patience, patience. The Harry Potter books will be on the rubbish piles, though after I myself are gone, and *Little, Big* will join the *Alice* books of Lewis Carroll and Kenneth Grahame's *The Wind in the Willows*.

As a literary critic who has covered the waterfront, for a while now, I find the mountain of mail that comes to me instructive, even though I cannot answer it, or even acknowledge it, if I myself am to go on reading, writing, teaching, and living. The two constant piles of vituperative missives come from Oxfordians, poor souls desperate to prove that Edward De Vere wrote all of Shakespeare, and Harry Potterites, of all ages and nationalities. The rage of the partisans of the Earl of Oxford, though crazy and unpleasant, baffles me less than the outrage of the legions of Potterites. Why are they so vulnerable to having their taste and judgment questioned?

No matter how fiercely we dumb down, led in this by *The New York Times Book Review* and the once-elite universities, period pieces seem to induce uneasy sensations in their contemporary enthusiasts. On tour in Turin, a year ago, I found myself talking about my *How to Read and Why* (Italian version) at an academy for writers called the Holden School, in honor of Salinger's hero. When the school's head, my host, a novelist, asked me why my book said nothing about *The Catcher in the Rye*, I gently intimated that I considered it a period piece, that would go on, perhaps for quite a while, but then would perish. Honest judgment has its costs, and I was shown out rather coldly when I departed. All critics, I know, are subject to error: my hero, Dr. Samuel Johnson, nodded in the terrible sentence: "*Tristam Shandy* did not last." And yet I wonder, as I age onwards, what it is in us that makes us so bitter when period pieces expire, if we are one of the survivors of a dead vogue?

JON A. YODER

The Muckraker

When the Statue of Liberty was dedicated in 1886, the poetic sentiments carved on its pedestal had already achieved the status of national mystique. But the response to the invitation went beyond the imaginations of the Founding Fathers who had identified America as a land offering liberty and justice for all. During the first ten years of this century, 8,795,386 immigrants entered the United States. Although 8,136,016 of the people came from Europe, less than a half million were from Great Britain, whereas the number included more than two million Italians and another two million from Austria and Hungary. Certainly the Pilgrims, despite seeing themselves as models to be emulated, would never have predicted that within a single decade 1,597,306 Russians would follow their example in choosing this New World.

Since he wanted to give a current report on the state of the American experiment, Sinclair's creation of a Lithuanian immigrant family was quite appropriate. For significant Russian immigration (including Lithuanians) was a recent phenomenon. In 1880 only five thousand Russians immigrated to the United States. But this number increased steadily until 1907, one year after *The Jungle* was published, when more than a quarter of a million Russians bet their lives that America was their promised land.

If these were new sorts of immigrants, they were coming for traditional economic and religious reasons. And Sinclair, who never separated

From *Upton Sinclair.* © 1975 by Frederick Ungar Publishing Co.

his economic condition from his spiritual or psychological state, was increasingly convinced that without socialism America could offer these new believers in the American Dream only a nightmarish existence. In 1905, while working on *The Jungle*, he took time to organize the Intercollegiate Socialist Society. Never again—if people like Sinclair, Jack London, Harry Laidler, and Norman Thomas could help it—would it be possible for someone to graduate from a university without being aware of the socialist solution. But it was his novel that called the attention of the world to Upton Sinclair. For his portrayal of Lithuanian peasants who come to America vividly suggests that our melting pot is less appetizing that the terms offered on our Statue of Liberty.

Jurgis Rudkis and Ona Lukoszaite, whose marriage in America constitutes the first chapter of *The Jungle*, had met in Brelovicz one and a half years earlier. It was true love at first sight, and "without ever having spoken a word to her, with no more than the exchange of half a dozen smiles, he found himself, purple in the face with embarrassment and terror, asking her parents to sell her to him for his wife." But Ona's father was rich and Jurgis was poor; so his application was denied. Then financial disaster struck the Lukoszaite family with the death of the father. Jurgis returned to find that "the prize was within his reach."

At the advice of Jonas, the brother of Ona's stepmother, they decide to go to America, "a place of which lovers and young people dreamed," a land where "rich or poor, a man was free." So the twelve Lithuanians—Jurgis and Ona, his father, her stepmother (and six children), Uncle Jonas, Cousin Marija—come to America, believing the advertisements about opportunities for anyone willing to work.

Throughout the first part of the book, Jurgis's response to increasing trouble is the one endorsed by Benjamin Franklin. When he finds that many of his wedding guests, especially the young ones, are abusing a time-honored custom by not contributing toward the costs of the affair he says, "I will work harder." When Ona panics at his suggestion that she take a day's honeymoon away from work "he answers her again: 'Leave it to me; leave it to me. I will earn more money—I will work harder.'"

The immigrants, as Sinclair describes them, are faced with the difficult task of retaining desirable aspects of an old way of life—their music, their religion, their concept of family—within a new setting that affords, supposedly, the chance to succeed economically via personal efforts. According to scholars such as Oscar Handlin, this effort was doomed to fail from the time they got on board the boat in Europe: "The qualities that were desirable in the good peasant were not those conducive to success in the transition. Neighborliness, obedience, respect, and status were valueless among the masses that struggled for space on the way."

Not only do old ways fall victim to new conditions in Sinclair's novel, but the promise of equal economic opportunity for which these old values were sacrificed turns out to be fraudulent. Again Handlin supports Sinclair's earlier analysis: "It was characteristic that, about then [1900], for every hundred dollars earned by native wage earners, the Italian-born earned eight-four, the Hungarians sixty-eight, and the other Europeans fifty-four."

Sinclair's title indicates that American society, in his analysis, had returned to the law of the jungle, where might makes right in a brutal survival of the fittest. But Sinclair was in no way one of those theorists who sought to apply the biological insights of Darwin to the realm of social relationships. John Higham has observed that "in their eagerness to convert social values into biological facts, Darwinian optimists unblinkingly read 'the fittest' to mean 'the best.'"

Sinclair directly opposed this. Rather than praising competition as a healthy and natural process—with cream always rising to the top—Sinclair accepted the contradictory value of cooperation. Competition, the socially inadequate law of the jungle, turns men into brutes in his novel:

> Every day the police net would drag hundreds of them off the streets, and in the Detention Hospital you might see them, herded together in a miniature inferno, with hideous, beastly faces, bloated and leprous with disease, laughing, shouting, screaming in all stages of drunkenness, barking like dogs, gibbering like apes, raving and tearing themselves in delirium.

Those who survived the dehumanizing competition inherent in capitalism were likely to be the least fit morally. Later, in *The Goslings*, Sinclair would refer to Yale's professor of political economy, William Graham Sumner (a leading Social Darwinist), as "a prime minister in the empire of plutocratic education." And what Sumner called an objective analysis of the way society had to operate was called by Sinclair the deification of the most brutish sort of selfishness, "covered by the mantle of science." In short, the classic Social Darwinist statement of John D. Rockefeller represents quite precisely those ideas that Sinclair felt were antithetical to the American Dream:

> The growth of a large business is merely a survival of the fittest. . . . The American Beauty rose can be produced in the splendor and fragrance which bring cheer to its beholder only by sacrificing the early buds which grow up around it. This is not an evil tendency in business. It is merely the working-out of a law of nature and a law of God.

In Sinclair's book, his version of reality, Jurgis cannot succeed finan-
cially without exchanging his high morality and willingness to work for a
cynical acceptance of the need to lie, cheat, steal, and exploit others. He gets
his first job in Packingtown—the name used to refer to the stockyards
district of Chicago—with ease, because he stands out as a fresh young stal-
wart among the rest of the applicants. Having completed a tour of his new
environment, he is prepared to face his first day's work with energetic enthusiasm: "He had dressed hogs himself in the forest of Lithuania; but he had
never expected to live to see one hog dressed by several hundred men. It was
like a wonderful poem to him, and he took it all in guilelessly."

With the whole clan contributing, Jurgis is able to put together enough
money for the down payment on a home—another opportunity they would
not have had in feudal Europe. But the contract is rigged so that if they ever
miss a payment they will lose the house. Jurgis eventually understands this,
and decides to work harder so that such a disaster will not occur. He makes
the same response when he discovers that his monthly payments do not
include the annual interest fee.

After one summer of work by the whole family, enough money is accumulated "for Jurgis and Ona to be married according to home traditions of
decency." But the first winter brings the first death. Jurgis's father contracts
a fatal disease, probably tuberculosis, from working in a filthy cellar.
Stanislovas, Ona's fourteen-year-old stepbrother, is a psychological victim of
the same winter. Although he continued to work at filling lard cans for five
cents per hour, he "conceived a terror of the cold that was almost a mania"
as a result of having seen his partner's frozen ears drop off when they were
rubbed too vigorously.

The financial contribution of Marija, who earned even more than
Jurgis by painting cans, stops without warning when the canning factory
closes for the winter. For Jurgis, too, winter is a slack season. Although he is
expected to be available at the "killing beds" all day, he is paid only for those
hours when he actually works; this system often reduces his income to about
thirty-five cents per day. In order to make the twelve-dollar monthly house
payment, meet the extra expenses of coal and winter clothing, and feed the
clan, Jurgis once again decides he will simply have to work harder.

Spring arrives, and so does a son, little Antanas. Ona develops "womb
trouble" from going back to work too quickly. But "the great majority of
the women who worked in Packingtown suffered in the same way, and from
the same cause, so it was not deemed a thing to see the doctor about."
Summer provides a chance to build up financial and physical reserves for
the second Chicago winter.

The first snowstorm hits just before Christmas, making it impossible
for the weakened Ona to walk to the spot on the line where she sewed hams

all day. But "the soul of Jurgis rose up within him like a sleeping lion." Starting out before dawn, he carries Ona through snowdrifts that come up to his armpits, repeating the performance around eleven o'clock every night.

But chance events can confound even the most physically fit. Upon occasion a steer would break loose on the killing beds, running amuck among workers who scramble over bloody floors to get behind pillars so that when "the floor boss would come rushing up with a rifle and begin blazing away" they could be counted among the survivors. During one such adventure Jurgis sprains his ankle and is unable to stand on his feet for two weeks. To make matters worse, Jonas, the brother of Ona's stepmother, decides that personal interests weigh more than family loyalty; he disappears, reducing the total income of the household while house payments remain constant.

Jurgis goes back to work before his ankle is healed, but he cannot function, so he loses his job. Now the family must try harder; the two younger brothers of Stanislovas, aged eleven and ten, become part of America's work force by selling newspapers. During this time one of the youngest children dies, probably from eating "tubercular pork that was condemned as unfit for export," but legal fare for Europeans who had come to America.

After two months Jurgis is able to walk again, but since he is no longer a prime physical specimen the only place in Packingtown where he can get a job is the fertilizer plant.

> To this part of the yards came all the "tankage," and the waste products of all sorts; here they dried out the bones—and in suffocating cellars, where the daylight never came, you might see men and women and children bending over whirling machines and sawing bits of bone into all sorts of shapes, breathing their lungs full of the fine dust, and doomed to die, every one of them, within a certain definite time.

Jurgis spends his third American summer there, and while he is able to make all of the house payments on time, his home falls apart. He and Ona have little to talk about, and they are generally too weary to care about each other. But remnants of old values remain. Thus when Jurgis discovers the following winter that Ona has slept with her boss in order to retain her job, he attacks the man viciously, gets himself thrown in jail for one month, and returns to find that the house is repainted—sold as new to brand-new victims.

He finally finds his family, lodged in the cheapest garret of a boarding-house, and enters to hear the screams of Ona dying in childbirth—an eighteen-year-old worn-out woman. He discovers that because of his attack on Ona's boss he is blacklisted, unable to work anywhere in Packingtown. This is almost overwhelming, but Jurgis's hopes are raised again when he finds relatively desirable work at the Harvester plant. The job lasts nine days; then the works are closed until further notice. He moves to a steel mill, works four days, and burns his hand so severely that he is laid off for more than a week. Then little Antanas drowns in the mud of Chicago's streets, and Jurgis becomes a cynic.

All this time Jurgis had been relatively successful in withstanding the temptation to escape his environment in the way chosen by most of the workers—alcohol. Now, rather than turning to drink, he decides to escape altogether. Jurgis walks out on the rest of Ona's relatives and becomes a hobo. When a farmer refuses to give him some food, he tears up one hundred young peach trees by the roots, thus demonstrating that he has adapted to America.

Jurgis wanders around the countryside for a summer, learning much about wine and women, and then returns to Chicago in the winter to help dig freight tunnels. A fight with a bartender leads to a second short jail term. But this time he makes friends with a professional thief who introduces Jurgis to the criminal underworld. Graduating from theft to political illegalities, Jurgis rises quite rapidly. He becomes a "foreman," placed back on the killing beds to insure the election of selected politicians every voting day.

Then a remnant of integrity from his past arises to plague him again. He meets Ona's old boss by chance and instinctively repeats his attack. His political friends are able to help him avoid a prison sentence, but he is now of little use to them and he must return to the life of a Chicago bum— stealing cabbages from grocers, drinking cheap beer for the sake of shelter, begging for funds to finance a night in a flophouse.

While begging, he discovers the address of Cousin Marija, who has become a prostitute. He visits her, hoping for some help, and learns that Stanislovas has been killed and eaten by rats after having been locked into his factory overnight by mistake.

Back on the street, Jurgis has no particular place to go, so in order to stay warm he enters a building in which a political rally is being held. He listens to a socialist speaker who correctly predicts that the "scales will fall from his eyes, the shackles will be torn from his limbs—he will leap up with a cry of thankfulness, he will stride forth a free man at last!"

Within a week of his conversion Jurgis finds a job at a small hotel run by a socialist. He begins to work at his new life with his old diligence. He reads much socialist literature and soon has enough money to support Ona's relatives again. (Marija, however, has become a dope addict, and "chooses" to remain a prostitute.) By the end of the novel Jurgis has become a thoroughly convinced socialist, part of the social movement that he and Sinclair expected to turn Chicago into a place fit for Americans.

Sinclair's novel is remembered, and rightly so, for its graphic descriptions of working conditions in Packingtown. But only about half of the book is concerned with the meat-packing industry, and even this half is used as a vehicle for Sinclair's larger message. What had happened to the spirit of America? What devil had tempted the American mind to substitute cash for value, thus allowing this intended Garden of Eden to go to seed—nourished by the heat of industrialization into a jungle of greed and grease and despair?

For Sinclair, bringing democracy to industry represented an answer to both economic and spiritual questions. He was not the first American to come to this conclusion. Earlier socialists, such as Edward Bellamy, had seen history as a working out of the gradual advance of the democratic principle. The Protestant Reformation had acknowledged all men as equal in status before God. The American and French Revolutions had introduced political equality. Now it was necessary to add economic equality in order to allow men their natural right to a human and fulfilling existence.

Sinclair (who believed this) was a muckraker determined to expose the inhumanity of capitalism so that Americans could opt for an economic system more closely aligned with their accepted ideals. Not all muckrakers had such extensive ideological motivations. According to Richard Hofstadter, most

> outstanding figures of the muckrake era were simply writers or reporters working on commission and eager to do well what was asked of them. A few, among them Upton Sinclair and Gustavus Myers, were animated by a deep-going dislike of the capitalist order, but most of them were hired into muckraking or directed toward it on the initiative of sales-conscious editors or publishers.

As Hofstadter demonstrates, "what was new in muckraking in the Progressive era was neither its ideas not its existence, but its reach—its nation-wide character and its capacity to draw nationwide attention. . . ." So there was an element of fad in the success of Sinclair's novel. But since his goal was to upset an irrational economic system, he was scarcely satisfied by causing a nation to regurgitate. In *Cosmopolitan Magazine* (October 1906) Sinclair wrote:

> Perhaps you will be surprised to be told that I failed in my purpose, when you know of all the uproar that "The Jungle" has been creating. But then that uproar is all accidental and was due to an entirely different cause. I wished to frighten the country by a picture of what its industrial masters were doing to their victims; entirely by chance I had stumbled on another discovery—what they were doing to the meat-supply of the civi-lized world. In other words, I aimed at the public's heart, and by accident I hit it in the stomach.

Two passages will suffice to show why the blow to the stomach was a direct hit:

> There were the wool pluckers, whose hands went to pieces even sooner than the hands of the pickle men; for the pelts of the sheep had to be painted with acid to loosen the wool, and then the pluckers had to pull out this wool with their bare hands, till the acid had eaten their fingers off. . . . As for the other men, who worked in the tank rooms full of steam, and in some of which there were open vats near the level of the floor, their peculiar trouble was that they fell into the vats; and when they were fished out, there was never enough of them left to be worth exhibiting—sometimes they would be overlooked for days, till all but the bones of them had gone out to the world as Durham's Pure Leaf Lard!

> There would be meat that had tumbled out on the floor, in the dirt and sawdust, where the workers had tramped and spit uncounted billions of consumption germs. There would be meat stored in great piles in rooms; and the water from leaky roofs would drip over it, and thousands of rats would race about on it. It was too dark in these storage places to see well, but a man could run his hand over these piles of meat and sweep up handfuls of the dried dung of rats. These rats were nuisances, and the packers would put poisoned bread out for them, they would die, and then rats, bread, and meat would go into the hoppers together. This is no fairy story and no joke. . . .

To treat it fairly then, *The Jungle* must be considered from two points of view. Historically, it provided the impetus for useful legislation. Few writers accomplish this, and it should be remembered that Sinclair's goal was to affect the lives of his readers. For an understanding of why Sinclair considered it a failure, however, the novel must be evaluated in terms of his larger purpose—converting a populace to democratic socialism. But first let us outline the impact of the successful social document.

Sinclair had trouble getting his dramatic statement onto center stage. Although it had been serialized by the *Appeal to Reason*, Sinclair wanted to reach an audience not already committed to socialism. Five publishers rejected it because, says Sinclair in his *Autobiography*, "nothing so horrible had ever been published in America—at least not by a respectable concern." The eventual publishers—Doubleday, Page & Co.—felt obliged to send their own lawyer, Thomas H. McKee, to investigate the industry before they risked publication. McKee's report supported Sinclair, and the book was published in February of 1906.

The Jungle immediately became the sensation of the day. The meat-packing scandal was front-page newspaper material for weeks, with Sinclair's name constantly attached. Supporting Hofstadter's contention that the only thing new about muckrakers was their ability to get attention, after Sinclair's exposé had aroused the nation and President Roosevelt, General Nelson Miller lamented the fact that outrage had come seven years too late for many Americans. He estimated that three thousand soldiers had died of "embalmed" beef during the Spanish-American War. But although he had collected the evidence and was prepared to produce two thousand witnesses, he could not find anyone in Congress who wished to open this particular can of worms.

Within a month the *Saturday Evening Post* published articles, signed by J. Ogden Armour, which defended the meat industry. The major packers, in Armour's view, were being falsely maligned. Actually, their impact upon America was benevolent, producing fresh and inexpensive meat as well as important byproducts used for medical research and glue. With respect to the cleanliness of America's meat, the defense was without qualification:

> In Armour & Co.'s business *not one atom of any condemned animal or carcass finds its way, directly or indirectly, from any source, into any food product or food ingredient.*
>
> Every meat animal and every carcass slaughtered in the Union Stockyards, or in the stock yards at any of the markets of the United States, is carefully inspected by the United States Government.

Readers were invited to believe that Government inspection "is the wall that stands between the meat-eating public and the sale of diseased meat."

Sinclair responded with a public statement in which he listed specific charges against Armour, openly inviting a libel suit so that the issues could be decided in a court of law. And in May, *Everybody's* published "The Condemned Meat Industry," in which Sinclair described at length the attempt to bribe Thomas F. Dolan, a former superintendent at Armour's & Co., who had signed an affidavit supporting Sinclair's claims. (Dolan accepted $5000 from Armour, and then published accounts of the bribe; let the buyer beware.) To Armour's contention that all meat was inspected, Sinclair added the information that this was to the benefit of foreign consumers only. Meat condemned by the federal officials could not be sold *abroad*.

Theodore Roosevelt, who was opposed to muckrakers in general, had eaten the army's canned meat in Cuba, so he was prepared to believe the worst. He invited Sinclair to Washington to discuss the issue, and he agreed to send Charles P. Neill (Labor Commissioner) and James B. Reynolds (Assistant Secretary of the Treasury) to Chicago to investigate.

The meat industry continued to maintain its assertions of purity. According to Congressman Wharton, representative of the meat-packing district in Chicago:

> The thing is all started from that book, and I know of my own knowledge that there is no foundation of fact in it. . . . I live in the packing district of Chicago. I know all about it. I know those packing houses as well as I know the corridors of the capitol. . . . Why, there is not a kitchen of a rich man in this city, or any other, that is any cleaner, if it is as clean, as those places.
>
> Of course, you know the sort of men many of the laborers in the packing houses are—foreigners of a low grade of intelligence—and you know how impossible it is control every individual. If those men happen to want to spit, they are likely to spit, but it doesn't go on the meat. This is nonsense. . . .

But the report of the federal investigators, kept secret at first (to Sinclair's public dismay), convinced President Roosevelt that present conditions were revolting. So he asked for a new law providing federal inspection for meat intended for domestic consumption. On 26 May 1906, the Senate passage of the Meat Inspection Bill was headlined in the New York *Times* as a "Direct Consequence of the Disclosures Made in Upton Sinclair's Novel." An amended House of Representatives version and the final compromise law were both passed in June of that year.

So Sinclair's success with *The Jungle*, on these terms, was significant. But it was not what he had in mind. It should be remembered that Sinclair wanted his writing to be very personal. *The Jungle*, in his opinion, was unlike the work of his contemporary producers of realistic literature because, as he wrote in *Cosmopolitan Magazine*, it was "written from the inside . . . the result of an attempt to combine the best of two widely different schools; to put the content of Shelley into the form of Zola." And Sinclair, personally, cared little about meat, since he rarely ate it.

But he did care deeply about what the meat industry typified and represented—the apparent failure on the part of American society to live up to established American ideals. The fact that his reading public responded to what he described as a symptom indicates his failure to communicate the more important concern about the basic illness.

Several explanations are supportable. Literature becomes impressive and memorable as it reduces abstract concepts to concrete examples. It is easier to remember that children's fingers, cows' fetuses, and rat dung, are the unlisted ingredients in deviled ham than that workers are oppressed, by definition, in a capitalist economy. Few readers, no matter how sympathetic, have found Sinclair's later chapters on socialist solutions to be as gripping as his preceding presentation of free enterprise at work. Through Jurgis, the reader learns about the advantages and imminence of socialism. But the speeches are tacked onto a plot that stops moving when Jurgis sits down to listen.

Sinclair, agreeing that the conclusion is weak, posits another explanation—one that fits in perfectly with his analysis of the intertwining of economic and spiritual concerns. He was too *poor* to turn his socialistic sermons into a more effective ending of *The Jungle*. In his *Autobiography* he writes: "The last chapters were not up to standard, because both my health and my money were gone, and a second trip to Chicago, which I had hoped to make, was out of the question."

In 1909 Sinclair again had reason to comment on the pernicious effect of money upon his career:

> Suffice it to say that never have I been able to write a single thing as I would have liked to write it, because of money. Either I was dead broke and had to rush it; or I knew that if I had my way, the public would not read it and the publishers would not accept it. Think of my having to ruin *The Jungle* with an ending so pitifully inadequate, because we were actually without money for food.

But even if philosophic solutions are harder to dramatize than scandalous situations, and even if Sinclair's efforts to make those solutions come to literary life were impeded by financial concerns, the public's positive response to Sinclair's described symptom (meat-packing conditions) while ignoring his deeper diagnosis (capitalistic greed), probably has more to do with audience than with author. If the story is read as exposing a scandal, a law can be passed, inspectors can be appointed to enforce that law, and we the people can receive a sense of continuing progress. This is far more palatable than reading the story as an indictment of one's entire way of life. To miss the basic point of any Sinclair writing requires strong motivation on the part of the reader. To look at what Sinclair was trying to teach is to discover what Americans were determined not to learn about themselves.

Beneath the rhetoric of a new society based on equality and brotherhood, America had built its experiment on tried and tested foundations of competition and greed. As indicated above, Jurgis personifies the willingness to accept individual responsibility for his own situation. He sets out across an ocean to solve his own problems through his own honest efforts; he wants to work. But by the turn of the century this point of view had become a demonstration of naiveté rather than of healthy optimism. Jurgis's co-laborers had already discovered that the game was rigged to allow only a few winners. So their response is the complete negation of the American Dream; they hate to work.

> They hated the bosses and they hated the owners; they hated the whole place, the whole neighborhood—even the whole city, with an all-inclusive hatred, bitter and fierce. Women and little children would fall to cursing about it; it was rotten, rotten as hell—everything was rotten.

For Sinclair, this undesirable result was built into the very theory of competitive capitalism:

> Here was Durham's, for instance, owned by a man who was trying to make as much money out of it as he could, and did not care in the least how he did it, and underneath him, ranged in ranks and grades like an army, were managers and superintendents and foremen, each one driving the man next below him and trying to squeeze out of him as much work as possible.

Men are not essentially evil, but within capitalism immoral behavior is systematically rewarded. Continuing his authorial comment in *The Jungle*, Sinclair contended:

> You could lay that down for a rule—if you met a man who was rising in Packingtown, you met a knave. . . . The man who told tales and spied upon his fellows would rise; but the man who minded his own business and did his work—why, they would "speed him up" till they had worn him out, and then they would throw him into the gutter.

Consequently, good men turn vicious in order to survive. Jurgis, who tries desperately to retain traditional values, yields to the stronger forces of inhumanity at the death of his son, "tearing up all the flowers from the garden of his soul, and setting his heel upon them." But Jurgis's creator retains those ideals, and he is in charge of the direction of the book. In his expression of very traditional American optimism, Sinclair believes that democracy will come to American industry because right eventually triumphs:

Those who lost in the struggle were generally exterminated; but now and then they had been known to save themselves by combination—which was a new and higher kind of strength. It was so that the gregarious animals had overcome the predaceous; it was so, in human history, that the people had mastered the kings. The workers were simply the citizens of industry, and the Socialist movement was the expression of their will to survive.

Sinclair's happy ending, the conversion of Jurgis to a rational method of social organization, is made complete and personal via a charge of emotional energy:

> The voice of Labor, despised and outraged; a mighty giant, lying prostrate—mountainous, colossal, but blinded, bound, and ignorant of his strength. And now a dream of resistance haunts him, hope battling with fear; until suddenly he stirs, and a fetter snaps—and a thrill shoots through him, to the farthest ends of his huge body, and in a flash the dream becomes an act! . . . He springs to his feet, he shouts in his new-born exultation—

Nothing could be more traditionally American than the belief that this happy ending was inevitable since God was counted on the good side of the struggle. Socialism, for Sinclair, "was the new religion of humanity—or you might say it was the fulfillment of the old religion, since it implied but the literal application of all the teachings of Christ." Filtering Tom Paine through Jonathan Edwards, Sinclair preaches about the redemption of "a man who was the world's first revolutionist, the true founder of the Socialist movement. . . . Who denounced in unmeasured terms the exploiters of his own time. . . . This union carpenter! This agitator, law-breaker, firebrand, anarchist!"

Answering the objection of those who do not believe in democratic socialism, Sinclair guaranteed the achievement of American equality through a rational distribution of wealth *without* totalitarian thought control:

> There was only one earth, and the quantity of material things was limited. Of intellectual and moral things, on the other hand, there was no limit, and one could have more without another's having less; hence "Communism in material production, anarchism in intellectual," was the formula of modern proletarian thought.

Sinclair's answer to the immigrants' problem applies the old solution, democracy, to the new conditions, industrialization and the emergence of mass man. Instead of the pathetic marriage of old immigrant values and new economic frustrations, Sinclair's solution insures that the survival of the fittest will also mean the perpetuation of the best. For example, Jurgis gets his first job as a socialist because a socialist employer has fired a man for drinking too much. The implication is clear; while the capitalist system drives a man to drink, if one drinks under socialism one *earns* dismissal.

The American people could have had all this, in Sinclair's opinion, simply by voting for their own interests. And they settled for federal meat inspection. But if most Americans were unwilling to risk actualization of traditional ideas, Sinclair was more than willing to test his theories by putting his new financial resources to work in an experiment in cooperative living.

Whatever the ultimate shortcomings of *The Jungle*, it gave Sinclair $30,000 with which to finance Helicon Home Colony—an experiment in which Sinclair had a very personal interest. As he wrote later, "because Meta was almost out of her mind, and I did not know what to do with David, I started Helicon Hall."

The property, which had previously been a boys' school, was described by the New York *Times* as palatial. It included a swimming pool, bowling alley, theater, and glass-protected tropical plants. Located on several acres of land in Englewood, New Jersey, the price was $36,000. Sinclair largely financed the effort, but other idealists were invited to contribute time, talent, and resources. Although plans called for hundreds of residents, twelve families spent the first winter in Helicon Hall, moving in on 1 November 1906. It was hoped that through experiment answers would evolve to some of the hotly debated questions of the day concerning childcare, diet, and the right of women to participate in making decisions.

In terms of public relations, Sinclair tried to emphasize the fact that this was only an effort at cooperative living, not a socialist colony. Anybody who believed, for example, that the usual methods of raising children, cooking food, and washing clothing were inefficient was invited to join—although a screening committee was set up to eliminate any applicants "whose habits and ideas would render them uncongenial." And with an eye toward compatibility, Sinclair's democratic ideals were compromised in the establishment of a rigid color line, "accepting the formula that the colony should be open to any white person of good moral character who is free from communicable disease."

Possibly the public reference to communicable disease stimulated speculation about the sexual habits of the residents. More likely, the national reputation of socialists as virile experimenters made inevitable the rumors that Sinclair was running a "free love" nest. The man who blushed at the contemplation of Renaissance art was, of course, righteously indignant when he responded to these allegations in his *Autobiography:* "I do not know of any assemblage of forty adult persons where a higher standard of sexual morals prevailed than at Helicon Hall."

Sinclair Lewis came to tend the furnace. William James and John Dewey visited, exchanging theories with the colonists about psychic phenomena and education. In addition to participation in discussions about liberalism versus anarchism, Sinclair wrote *The Industrial Republic*, a book of prophecy that anticipated a social revolution "in America within one year after the Presidential election of 1912." The period spent in Helicon Hall was, in short, an optimistic time during which, Sinclair tells us in his *Autobiography*, "the young dreamer of Utopia lived according to his dreams." Then on 7 March 1907, Sinclair awakened to find Helicon Home Colony on fire. He escaped, to stand outside in the snow, watching the "beautiful utopia flame and roar, until it crashed in and died away to a dull glow."

After the rubble and the debts were cleared away, Sinclair returned to the familiar but unhappy state of affairs that had preceded publication of *The Jungle*. Stomach trouble and headaches returned with destitution. Meta almost died of appendicitis and was sent to a sanitarium in Battle Creek, Michigan, for recovery. Upton joined her there later, and as a result of the argumentation of Dr. W. K. Kellogg—not as a result of his work on *The Jungle*—he became a vegetarian.

Very much interested in the health of his family, Sinclair decided to move to Bermuda for the winter of 1907–08. A publisher's advance for *The Metropolis* financed the trip, but poor sales meant Sinclair had to borrow money to return to the United States. *The Millennium*, a drama written in Bermuda, and *The Moneychangers* (a novel written as a sequel to *The Metropolis*) produced no significant interest and hardly enough income to cover Sinclair's minimal expenses. So when he received invitations to come to California from Gaylord Wilshire (the socialist gold miner) and poet George Sterling, Sinclair "set out over the pathway of the argonauts in a Pullman car."

Sinclair stopped at Chicago for a socialist rally, then moved on to the University of Kansas, where he wanted to meet a young writer with whom he had been corresponding. Sinclair was quite convinced that Harry Kemp would become the next great American poet. In fact, Kemp was to become the man whose relationship with Meta would provide scandalous copy for American gossip columns. In 1911, when Sinclair announced that he was going to seek a divorce, he was to blame Kemp with "influencing" Meta in the wrong ways.

Sinclair spent the winter of 1908–09 in California, writing plays and trying to keep Sterling from drinking. (Meta was in New York with David, who had tonsillitis.) But by the spring of 1909, he and Meta agreed to try living together again. They met in Florida, neutral territory, moved to Long Island for the summer, and then went back to Battle Creek for the discovery of health through fasting, as described in *The Fasting Cure* (1911). Harry Kemp arrived to visit Upton, and while Harry was becoming interested in Meta, Sinclair made the acquaintance of Mary Craig Kimbrough, a twenty-five-year-old Southern belle from Mississippi.

Still interested in utopian experiments, Sinclair then moved his family to a single-tax colony in Alabama. Shortly thereafter, agreeing to a divorce, Meta moved back north, leaving David with his father. Sinclair was writing his troubles into *Love's Pilgrimage* (1911), a book described in his *Autobiography* as "a novel about modern marriage that would show the possibility of a couple's agreeing to part, and still remaining friends."

In the spring of 1910 Upton and David Sinclair moved to another single-tax colony in Delaware. Meta joined them there, occupying one of three tents "on a strictly literary basis," until she moved south to help Mary Craig Kimbrough write a novel about the daughter of Jefferson Davis. Then Harry Kemp and George Sterling went east to visit at the same time as Meta and Mary Craig went north to negotiate with publishers, and the stage was set for a public divorce scandal.

Sinclair, the notorious troublemaker, was subjected to vicious analyses of his own troubles. In *The Brass Check* he reports that the "generally accepted explanation was that I had married an innocent young girl and taught her 'free love' doctrines, and then, when she practiced these doctrines, I kicked her out of my home." Sinclair's own explanation, thinly fictionalized in *Love's Pilgrimage*, is less sensational but more perceptive. He has Thyrsis write a letter to Mr. Hardin, Corydon's new love:

> I suppose there is no need for me to tell you that Corydon is not happy. She never has been happy as my wife, and I fear she never will be. She is by nature warm-hearted, craving affection and companionship. I, on the other hand, am by nature impersonal and self-absorbed—I am compelled by the exigencies of my work to be abstracted and indifferent to things about me. . . . If in the course of time it should become clear that Corydon would be happier as your wife than as mine, I should regard it as my duty to step aside.

But divorces were granted more easily by Thyrsis than by Catholic judges in New York at that time. So in 1912 Sinclair went to Amsterdam where "the husband was not required to prove that he had beaten or choked

or poisoned his wife; he might receive a divorce on the basis of a signed statement by the wife, admitting infidelity."

Mary Craig followed Sinclair to the Netherlands, but their developing
relationship was complicated by the awareness that Upton's friend, George
Sterling, loved her too. Sterling wrote more than one hundred sonnets
(which Sinclair later edited) to the woman whose "heart had been broken by
an early love affair at home; she knew she would never love again." But she
did, and then she persuaded her aristocratic father that she ought to marry a
divorced man.

So the daughter of a Mississippi banker married the socialist muckraker
on 21 April 1913. Until her death in 1961, Mary Craig was Sinclair's constant
companion, providing consistent ideological support for an author whose
personal life was always a large part of his writing. This new marital situation
provided the stability necessary for the continuing stream of liberal argument Sinclair was now prepared to address to an American public—a reading
audience that had misunderstood his first significant novel but that would be
given many more chances to see how apparently dying American values
could be revitalized.

MICHAEL BREWSTER FOLSOM

Upton Sinclair's Escape from The Jungle: The Narrative Strategy and Suppressed Conclusion of America's First Proletarian Novel

When Upton Sinclair committed himself to writing *The Jungle*, he had no idea how he was going to pull it off, and he ended up improvising all the way. The result was a novel, the first ever to be called "proletarian," which is far more complex and revealing than is generally understood. We still tend to break the book in two, and read it, as its first public did, for the sensational early chapters, dismissing the rest as a tedious tract. However, taken whole, in light of the story of its conception, composition, and revision, *The Jungle* comes to look less like an episode in the muckrake movement, and more like a major text of American social fiction, one of those compelling, garbled, perplexing, sometimes amusing encounters between the conventionally literate and the working class, which became a fixture of imaginative life in America by the end of the nineteenth century.

Just what Sinclair brought to this encounter, in the way of experience and assumption, is necessary and not too difficult to determine. Before, during, and after publication of *The Jungle*, Sinclair explained at length—perhaps too much—about his background and his approach to his new materials.

We must first appreciate that Sinclair was an extraordinarily serious writer, for this determined not only the protestant severity of his tone, but also the character of his politics and the resolution of his plot. *The Jungle* was to be serious literature—*great* literature, Sinclair assumed—not the

From *Prospects: An Annual of American Cultural Studies*. © 1979 by Burt Franklin & Co., Inc. and Jack Salzman.

commercial pulp he had written so much of already. He concluded one of several articles defending his veracity by explaining how hard and how long he had been in training to write *The Jungle*. There had been fifteen years of study (that is, since age twelve), five million words already written and published, four or five thousand books read, "including all the worth while novels in . . . five languages," and many other chores besides, all at a computed cost of $20,000. No packinghouse worker would ever have had the money and leisure to acquire such skills, he argued. Quite the contrary. Thought there are indeed many people in the stockyards who feel as their author does, "their knowledge is no avail, for they cannot write novels; if they have ever written anything at all it has been some pitiful cry which has appeared in some obscure socialist newspaper." Such effete professionalism swelled to a crescendo of self-advertisement. The article concludes:

> The people of Packingtown had to wait for their deliverance upon the strange coincidence of a novelist who had all the training which the schools could give him, but was so bent upon writing things which the world did not want to read that he was willing for himself and his whole family to descend into the social pit and to experience all the degradation, physical, mental, and moral of the wages-slaves of the stockyards; and who then had left enough strength and iron resolve to gather himself together, and take his life upon the final cast, and put it all into a book into "one terrible, heart-rending, menacing cry materialized in black and white, the anguish of a great multitude made articulate." I quote the words from the review of *Life*, which seems to me to cover the case.

The genial, well-intentioned, hyperbolical insolence of the man contrasts sharply with his actual successes in sympathetically and credibly representing the lives of working people, though it finally got the better of his art and his politics, as I shall argue. The point here is to appreciate the sense of mission with which he approached his work on *The Jungle*.

By the time he started *The Jungle*, which was within a year of his actually becoming a Socialist, Sinclair had worked out a rudimentary theory of literature to define what a radical novelist should be concerned with. In October 1904, as he was heading to Chicago to gather material for *The Jungle*, he published an article in *Collier's* on the problems of contemporary literature, with the promising title, "Our Bourgeois Literature—The Reason and the Remedy." In that article, Sinclair proposed a strict determinist view of the relation of literature and society: "The literature of any civilization [is] simply the index and mirror of that civilization." American literature is "timid," "materialistic," and "anemic" because it tallies with the needs and character of the reigning middle class. But, Sinclair continued, bourgeois civilization is torn by class conflict, and the mirror of literature reflects the working-class side as well, especially in the United States, where "the terrific forces of [modern civilization] have reached their highest intensity; it is here that men are most pressed and molded by them, that the ideals and passions of the industrial battle find their fullest and most vehement expression."

Sinclair's roster of those writers who had been expressing these ideals and passions was a catholic pantheon, which indicates that Sinclair was making no special brief for realism. His list of "Socialist" writers included Björnsen, Maeterlinck, Sudermann, Hauptmann, Ibsen, Tolstoy, Zola, Gorky, "even Mr. Bernard Shaw" (but not William Morris); in the United States there were Howells, Markham, Bruno Lessing, Bliss Carmen, Richard Le Gallienne, Jack London, and "the followers of Emerson and Whittier, of Lincoln, Wendell Phillips and every other freedom-loving man we ever had."

Concerning the representation of life on the working-class side of the battle lines, Sinclair mocked the complacent and "entertaining" writers who "may even go to the slums and show us the ways of Mrs. Wiggs, her patient frugality and beautiful contentment in that state of life to which it has pleased God to call her." And he suggested, but did not assert, that it may be valuable to explore in a literary way "the wilds and jungles of the cities of civilized man." But he did not really argue that the way to remedy the "bourgeois" malaise of literature is to infuse it with the actual character, culture, and life-style of the slums. He did not make an anti-bourgeois virtue out of the "frankness" and "honest" dirt of urban poverty, as some American radicals already were doing in the first years of the century. At the moment when he himself was about to head for the slums, he was arguing for an aesthetic that shared with conventional literature a partiality toward moral and sentimental abstractions. Sinclair was interested in "the ideals and passions of the industrial battle." He looked to a future that promised "the entering of humanity upon its real task, the spiritual life."

Just how Sinclair found himself on the working-class side of the "industrial battle," qualified to appreciate and articulate "the anguish of a great multitude," was one of his favorite themes. He had, indeed, been poor himself—very poor—though the style of his poverty was rather more respectable than that which he discovered among Eastern European immigrants in Packingtown. In social and economic origin, Sinclair was déclassé Southern gentry—Anglo-Saxon, Protestant (Episcopal), and with Confederate naval officers and successful commercial gentlemen among his forebears. His father, however, was an alcoholic. Sinclair saw the possibilities of wealth and leisure through the eyes of a poor relation, whose life was

. . . a series of Cinderella transformations; one night sleeping on a vermin-ridden sofa in a lodging house, and the next night under silken coverlets in a fashionable home. It was always a question of one thing—whether my father had the money for that week's board. If he didn't my mother paid a visit to her father, the railroad official.

Sinclair's early literary career was also a period of want. His first serious novels did not earn nearly enough to support him, even given his own ascetic standards, and in public he was pleased to call himself a "would-be singer and penniless rat." In his autobiography, Sinclair insists:

Externally, the story [*The Jungle*] had to do with a family of stockyard workers, but internally it was the story of my own family. Did I wish to know how the poor suffered in wintertime in Chicago? I had only to recall the previous winter in the cabin, when we had only cotton blankets, and had put rugs on top of us.

One should not underestimate the profundity of the anguish Sinclair experienced, psychic as much as physical, when he subjected his wife and baby to penury for the sake of his art. The shame of the poor relation added to the vehemence of a "prophetic" passage in the largely autobiographical *Journal of Arthur Stirling* (1902), one of Sinclair's first serious fictions. There, his likeness, the foiled poet Stirling, rants:

The boarding houses that I have lived in! . . . The landladies' faces—the assorted stenches—the dark hallways—the grabbing, quarreling, filthy, beer-carrying tenants . . . of those experiences I could make myself another Zola. . . . Some day I shall put into a book all the rage and all the hate and all the infamy of these things.

Sinclair encountered industrial Chicago not only with a sense of privation and a program for eradicating it, but with a sensibility remarkable in an American writer at the turn of this century, a taste for the terms and conditions of working-class experience, which inspired the contumely of many a squeamish reviewer. At his best, Sinclair was able to ask the reader to cope with the squalor of industrial civilization as its victims do, often with equanimity. At the same time, Sinclair sought to turn the representation of squalor into a persuasive argument for revolutionary action which would abolish that same squalor. This resulted, at times, in a complex interrelation between tough sensibility and stiff ideology, which called for simultaneous acceptance and rejection of the way things are. And through all this, Sinclair appeared to share the point of view and sensibility of his working-class characters.

A good example of this complex perception of working-class experience is the lavishly sensuous introduction of Jurgis and his immigrant party to Chicago. Sinclair was dubious, speculative, even appreciative. As the immigrants approach Chicago by train,

> . . . along with the thickening smoke they began to notice another circumstance, a strange, pungent odor. They were not sure that it was unpleasant, this odor; some might have called it sickening . . . they were only sure that it was curious.

Sinclair acknowledged the possibility of objection ("some" would consider it "sickening"), but he went on to stress the lack of certainty. The members of the party "were divided in their opinions about it." "There were some who drank it in as if it were an intoxicant; there were others who put their handkerchiefs to their faces." But the sensual vigor of the experience prevails: "The new immigrants were tasting it, lost in wonder. . . . It was an elemental odor, raw and crude; it was rich, almost rancid, sensual, and strong."

There had never been anything like this almost fond response to offal, hot flesh, and manure in the literature of poverty, and Sinclair kept it up for a while. The smoke returns to sight. Standing on a Chicago street, the newcomers see a "vista":

> . . . half a dozen chimneys, tall as the tallest of buildings, touching the very sky—and leaping from them half a dozen columns of smoke, thick, oily, and black as night. It might have been from the center of the world, this smoke, where the first of the ages still smolder. It came as if self-impelled, driving all before it, a perpetual explosion.

There is something here of the naturalist formula for endowing manmade events with "value-free" significance and "natural" (nonhuman) origins. (Sinclair's tendency in this direction crops up again in the pastoral episode in Chapter 22.) The net effect here is to make the smoke of industry (and, by association, industry itself) merely a fact of life, rather than a literal enemy or a symbol or portent of disaster. Similarly, the sounds of Packingtown—the "distant lowing of ten thousand cattle, the distant grunting of ten thousand swine," which the immigrants first hear—Sinclair rendered familiar, almost intimate, while acknowledging its capacity to distress:

This, too, like the odor, was a thing elemental. . . . You scarcely noticed it at first—it sunk into your consciousness, a vague disturbance, a trouble. It was like the murmuring of the bees in the spring, the whisperings of the forest; it suggested endless activity, the rumblings of a world in motion.

Sinclair closed his immigrants' first day in Chicago with sensations he must have felt himself:

The line of the buildings stood clear-cut and black against the sky; here and there out of the mass rose the great chimneys, with the river of smoke streaming away to the end of the world. It was a study in colors now, this smoke; in the sunset light it was black and brown and gray and purple. All the sordid suggestions of the place were gone—in the twilight it was a vision of power . . . it seemed a dream of wonder, with its tale of human energy, of things being done, of employment for thousands of men, of opportunity and freedom, of life and love and joy.

Sinclair often vexed his reader with the ugliness of this world and viciousness of human relations engendered by it, but he was also capable of seeing all that is ugly and vicious swept aside by the "visions of power, "dream of wonder," and "tale of human energy."

Among the novelists of industrial civilization, Sinclair had the advantage, shared by none before him, and few afterwards, of enjoying and approving the industrial mode of production. Twenty years after *The Jungle* appeared, Sinclair put his position forcefully in *Mammonart*, his hasty tour through all of Western literature. Explaining his differences with William Morris on the matter of art and industry, he noted that *News from Nowhere* is a reply to *Looking Backward*, which Morris "did not like, . . . because Bellamy was an American, and had organized and systematized every-thing." Sinclair was pleased to identify himself with things organized, systematized, and, thus, American: "I am a Socialist who believes in machinery, and has no interest in any world that does not develop machine power to the greatest extent." The eyes of Morris and Ruskin were "blinded by smoke," Sinclair insisted:

There is no reason why machines should not make beautiful and substantial things, instead of making ugly and dishonest things— except the fact that the machines are owned by people who have no interest except to make a profit out of the product.

In *The Jungle*, Sinclair departed even further from the vision of Morris; he was not at all concerned with the capacity of machines to beautify the world, but rather with the efficiency and power—even the beauty—of men and machines organized together in an essentially ugly (but necessary) business.

As we are introduced to the methods of the stockyards in company with Jurgis and the other immigrants, we might almost be in the hands of Armour's public relations department. The new arrivals are in constant "wonder" at the order and efficiency of it all, how nothing is wasted. Sinclair gave a lengthy, detailed description of the several methods of dispatching livestock and the ways the carcasses are transmuted into a plenitude of products. Not differentiating himself from his characters, Sinclair remarked at one point, "It was all so very businesslike that one watched it fascinated. It was pork-making by machinery, pork-making by applied mathematics."

Sinclair did indulge in some humane tremulation, reflecting that the "innocent" pigs are dealt with in such a "cold-blooded, impersonal way, without a pretense at apology, without the homage of a tear." And, this time distinguishing himself from his immigrants who "were not poetical," Sinclair waxed poetical: "One could not stand and watch very long without becoming philosophical, without beginning to deal in symbols and similes, and to hear the hog-squeal of the universe." But this is "the greatest aggregation of labor and capital ever gathered in one place," and that is a marvel.

Jurgis and his company do not stand and watch reflectively, but react as participants. Jurgis goes on a tour of the slaughterhouses, conscious that he has already got a job, and has "become a sharer in all this activity, a cog in all this marvellous machine," which seemed "a thing as tremendous as the universe—the laws and ways of its working no more than the universe to be questioned or understood." To work hard and be paid for it decently means dignity, freedom, and joy.

Now, of course, Sinclair was setting out to question the laws and ways of the meat packers' works, and he used Jurgis' initial innocence and gradual disillusionment as foil and technique of discovery. But the one thing that Sinclair never questioned is the essential organization of large industry, the minute division of labor which determines that each hand shall repeat one small act of the whole task all day long. (This acceptance and even appreciation of mass production is reemphasized in the episodes of Jurgis' employment in a harvester works [Chapter 20] and in a steel mill [Chapter 21].) One of the reasons Sinclair could identify with the working poor is that he accepted manual labor as an occupation with real satisfactions. He was writing about hard and brutal toil. Jurgis likes to sweat, for that is proof of his manhood (just as Sinclair sought to justify himself through compulsive, blinkered, and unremitting literary labors). Sweat is all Jurgis knows how to do, and he is not to be pitied or condescended to for being an honest working man, happy to be earning 17½¢ an hour shoveling guts: "It was not the pleasantest work one could think of, but it was necessary work, and what more had a man the right to ask then a chance to do something useful, and get good pay for doing it?" The innocence of Jurgis' delight in his work is soon undercut by all kinds of rude afflictions and disillusionments. But even after Sinclair thoroughly revealed the disaster of working-class life, he returned to the theme of a person's satisfaction in labor. Thus, much later in the novel, when Jurgis has been given a menial job in a steel mill, Sinclair writes:

> It was wonderful, when one came to think of it, that these men should have taken an interest in the work they did; they had no share in it—they were paid by the hour, and paid no more for being interested. Also they knew that if they were hurt they would be flung aside and forgotten—still they would hurry to their task by dangerous short-cuts, would use methods that were quicker and more effective in spite of the fact that they were also risky.

Just how to make a novel out of such experience was another problem entirely, as Sinclair was ready to admit. He was uncertain about what kind of novel he would write. Indeed, the work started out not as a novel but as an act of concerted social and economic *research*. Afterward, Sinclair was even uncertain about the extent to which what he had written was, indeed, a novel.

Sinclair's reason for writing a work about the Chicago stockyards was that a recent, unsuccessful strike there had brought the subject to his attention. With a $500 advance from the Socialist weekly *Appeal to Reason*, in the autumn of 1904, he spent seven weeks in and around the Chicago stockyards. Most of the succeeding winter and spring he composed his fiction, for serial publication in the *Appeal*. The researcher's approach was not only the basis of the fiction but also in some ways the very soul of it. Sinclair's intention was to write a book that would be realistic, not just in its representation of the character, nature, and relations of people, their institutions and scenery, but also true to the situation he himself had observed—only somewhat compressed, reordered, and slightly veiled to suit what he though were the minimum requirements of a fictional narrative. Sinclair put it this way: "As a writer of fiction I could be required to be true only in the way of art, and not in the way of a newspaper; but, as it happened, I was able to be true in both ways, and the book might as well have the credit for it." What Sinclair may have meant by and done about being "true in the way of art" must be considered, but he himself was led to emphasize the "newspaper" truth of his work:

I intend "The Jungle" to be an exact and faithful picture of the conditions as they exist in Packingtown, Chicago. I mean it to be true, not merely in substance, but in detail, and in the smallest detail. It is as true as it should be if it were not a work of fiction at all, but a study by a sociologist; it is so true that students may go to it, as they would to a work of reference.

In the strenuousness of his defense of his facts, Sinclair went so exceedingly far as to deny the very imaginative basis of the work altogether: "I have exercised none of the ordinary privileges of the writer of fiction. I have imagined nothing, I have embellished nothing; I have simply dramatized and interpreted." In other situations, Sinclair indicated that he knew better. Still, it is evident that for him fiction served fact, and was, in the case of *The Jungle*, subsequent in the process of creation. In his *Autobiography*, Sinclair recalled that "at the end of a month or more [in Chicago], I had my data and knew the story I meant to tell, but I had no characters." He explained that he accidentally stumbled upon a Lithuanian wedding feast in progress. He sat watching the participants late into the night, and came away with the narrative formed and fleshed out in memory. In a much earlier account, Sinclair suggested that the overall conception of the narrative, not just the characters for an already framed tale, grew out of that chance experience: "I watched the people there and imagined their lives, and little by little the whole story took shape. Everything I had previously planned seemed in some miraculous way to fit in with them."

Just what that "whole story" would be was hardly settled in the epiphany of that Chicago evening, and the story that did take shape in Sinclair's fancy was rather different from the exposé of the packing industry, which casual readers usually recall. The narrative is significantly more elaborate and complex. Indeed, the novel we have is very different from the one Sinclair first conceived.

To arouse interest in his forthcoming serial, Sinclair published a précis of his promised work two weeks before the first installment appeared. He was emphatic about his sentimental appeal. The novel would "set forth the breaking of human hearts." It would "break the popular heart." It would be a "heart-breaking tragedy." But it would not preach. "What Socialism there will be in this book, will, of course, be imminent [*sic*]; it will be revealed by incidents—there will be no sermons." "The scene will be Chicago and the stockyards strike," Sinclair writes.

I have been there and seen things. But I did not have to go to Chicago to learn of the struggle and of the mental and physical breakdown which follows. There will be factories and bad air and accidents and adulterated food. All around will be strikes and employer's associates and grafting politicians—and Socialists. The reader will get glimpses of various tragedies; there will be, perhaps, a bit of the white slave traffic. There will be foreigners who have come to America to find liberty, and are out of work. . . . As I said, I will write this book to be read. In the climax of the strike the hero's wife will give birth to a child. She will be unattended and unless I am mistaken, I can make a fruitful tragedy out of this by relating the simple truth, without transgressing proprieties. The strike fails, the hero is not taken back; his wife is evicted and dies. He tends the baby a while, feeds it on poisoned milk and impure drugs, and finally it dies also. Then the hero goes out and hears about anarchism. Anarchists and the social crime and terror that make them have not yet been put into fiction. The hero is making bombs—and then he learns about Socialism. He meets a man—a poor, hunger driven tailor—a Socialist—one of the real heroes of the social revolution—who suddenly causes the whole of the problem to become clear to him—who flashes a light into the farthest depth of the "jungle."

The précis suggests a narrative economy and a breadth of political exploration to which Sinclair did not hold. In the novel Jurgis does not become involved in a climactic strike in the way suggested. There is no anarchist episode. The introduction to socialism is much attenuated—and founded upon a sermon. This précis suggests no conclusion of a plot. Indeed, that was to prove Sinclair's biggest difficulty in the months to come.

Sinclair had certainly not completed his work by the time he started serial publication in *Appeal to Reason* in late February 1905. As the story turned out, Jurgis' stint as a packinghouse worker is over by the end of Chapter 15 (there were thirty-six in the serial version). His wife and child are dead, and all ties to the world of the wedding feast are cut two-thirds of the way through the narrative. Jurgis' fortunes even have several rather good turns after he leaves the yards and loses his family. There is the spell of work in the South Chicago steel mill, and another in the harvester works. There is good money in small crime and employment as a politician's tool or scab foreman in the strikebound yards. There is a significant pastoral episode (Chapter 22) in which Jurgis and Sinclair try out agrarian alternatives to the industrial disaster, and much more that Sinclair had evidently not conceived when he started writing—and publishing—his novel.

The serial form to which he had committed himself posed problems he had not anticipated. It was a form he was well practiced at, for he had written many a boy's magazine adventure tale. But *The Jungle* does not read like serial fiction, and Sinclair became aware of his difficulty very soon.

He wanted to write fiction that was serious yet popular, Socialist yet popularly successful. And he wanted to do this while he was introducing new subject matter into American fiction. The problem, as he first perceived it, was that even a Socialist audience was ignorant of the world of urban poverty. The *Appeal to Reason* had a larger working-class Socialist readership than any publication in the history of the American left—its circulation was close to 300,000 during the months *The Jungle* appeared. Sinclair addressed this audience directly in an open letter to "Comrades of the Appeal," a week after his first installment was published. He described the melodramatic conventions of serial fiction, and wondered if, missing them, his readers might not give up *The Jungle* in despair. But he hoped his readers would understand his serious purposes. He was intending to write a story with "climaxes" and "things happening," to be sure, but "I want these things to be real and convincing, and not superficial. That means, as I conceive it, that I have first to make the reader acquainted with an atmosphere and environment, and that takes time." Sinclair continued, "the reader must first have the system in his mind; and concerning the system that prevails in Packingtown, the average American is as ignorant as an unborn babe. My belief is that the majority of the *Appeal* readers are ignorant of it." Having made his apology, Sinclair seems to have simply ignored the problem thereafter, for the narrative continues to bear little evidence of the conventions of serial fiction.

Another anticipated difficulty soon faced Sinclair in the matter of literary decorum. Many of the things Sinclair intended to make "real and convincing" were not admissible in polite literature—the squalor, ugliness, sometimes depravity of working-class life, and the facts of sexuality. Sinclair started out intending to respect the conventions of polite literature. In the précis of the novel to come, printed in the *Appeal*, he promised to represent Ona's death in childbirth: "unless I am mistaken, I can make a fruitful tragedy out of this by relating the simple truth, without transgressing proprieties." But he was mistaken, for much that is satisfactory about the novel, including the grotesque episode of Ona's death, results from Sinclair's need to transgress convention and to force into American fiction crucial matter its practitioners had excluded. Not long into his narrative, Sinclair broke away for a reflective moment to confront one problem of literary etiquette directly:

There is a poet who sings that

> Deeper their heart grows and nobler their bearing,
> Whose youth in the firest of anguish hath died.

But it is not likely that he had reference to the kind of anguish that comes with destitution, that is so endlessly bitter and cruel, and yet so sordid and petty, so ugly, so humiliating—unredeemed by the slightest touch of dignity or even of pathos.

Sinclair went on to state specifically the incongruence between such matter and the conventions of literature and its accustomed audience:

> It is a kind of anguish that poets have not commonly dealt with; its very words are not admitted into the vocabulary of poets—the details of it cannot be told in polite society at all. How, for instance, could anyone expect to excite sympathy among lovers of good literature by telling how a family found their home alive with vermin, and of all the suffering and inconvenience and humiliation they were put to, and the hard-earned money they spent, in efforts to get rid of them?

The lightly mocking phrase "lovers of good literature" is synonymous with "polite society," and the "language of poets" must be acceptable to both. And Upton Sinclair came to defy them all, with the same bluff insolence and ingenuousness he drew upon when telling Theodore Roosevelt how to run his country. Sinclair concluded the paragraph about vermin with a patient explanation of exactly how much the insecticide they bought cost, what its precise chemical constituents were, and how ineffective it was.

By the time Sinclair had finished his story and had become famous, he was able to restate his original intention with respect to the "proprieties." At the height of his notoriety, he boasted that all along, he had "meant to tell the truth, and to tell it relentlessly, and without in any way considering conventions or proprieties." Unhappily, his accomplishments could not be sustained. Sinclair never wrote so well again, and we should not be surprised, for *The Jungle* itself, despite its successes in realism, fell victim to conventions and proprieties more fundamental than (though allied to) those of polite literature. As Sinclair worked out his plot during months of crisis in his personal, political, and imaginative life, the great gulf widened between Sinclair, the expensively educated professional writer, and the humble working stiffs who peopled his brilliant early chapters. The Anglo-Saxon Protestant petit-bourgeois intellectual triumphed over realism, Socialism, the alien working class, and serious literature.

By the summer of 1905, Sinclair was in real trouble. The drift of his plot was increasingly unsatisfactory, for reasons Leon Harris, Sinclair's recent biographer, suggests:

> This reader of Shelley, even though he had read Zola, . . . was not prepared for the obvious hopelessness of the lives of his characters. Therefore, . . . [he] found himself paralyzed; for the first time in his life he was unable to write and so incapable of finishing the book.
>
> In Upton's half-dime-novel days, any sort of *deus ex machina* would have done to end *The Jungle*—but no longer.

Sinclair was in more than literary trouble. His relations with his first wife, Meta, were deteriorating. An experiment in self-sufficient homesteading was a disappointment. The $500 the *Appeal* had advanced him was long spent, as was the $500 George Brett of Macmillan had advanced for rights to a book version of *The Jungle*. The peculiarities of the last third of the novel can be laid, in part, to desperation, both economic and literary.

Sinclair was sufficiently desperate at the beginning of the summer to suggest in a letter to Brett that he would consider capitulating to demands that he pull his punches: "The subject of the publishability of certain parts of the ms.," he wrote, "is open for debate." He told Brett, "I have only 27 cents in my pocket. . . . Nevertheless I am going on writing this afternoon."

Brett was unmoved by pleas for an additional advance, and Sinclair's immediate solution to his difficulties was not to go on writing at all. For the better part of the summer of 1905, while previously composed installments of *The Jungle* continued to appear regularly in the *Appeal*, Sinclair gave up all attempts at finishing the novel and threw himself into more practical political activity—organizing the intercollegiate Socialist Society. By early September he could enjoy some encouraging results. The respite from writing and the political self-confirmation may well have been crucial in freeing him to complete his political fiction. But many complications remained. His final extravagant, desperate, irresolute tinkerings with his plot show him at the mercy of his publishers, his uncertainties, his vainglorious notions of his importance. Sinclair ultimately moved to resolve his difficulties by suppressing the disagreeable possibilities that his experience of working-class life led him into.

"I did the best I could," Sinclair wrote in a genial retrospect, "and those critics who didn't like the ending ought to have seen it as it was in manuscript." Sinclair's first solution was to avoid, or at least postpone, concluding the novel altogether. In September, when he seems to have had this monstrous draft manuscript done, he wrote George Brett acknowledging his difficulties:

> I think that the incidents in the second half of my book move too swiftly and that its characters are insufficiently realized. The reasons for the fault were, first my exhaustion, and secondly my desire to keep the book from stretching to an unpublishable length, and thirdly, my comparative unfamiliarity with the rest of Chicago—except Packingtown, that is.

And he offered Brett an interesting proposal, a "definite proposition, . . . which is final, so far as I am concerned." That was to publish "as 'The Jungle' of our contract" the work as he had written it through the death of Ona. He then suggested that Brett advance him another $500.

> . . . to complete a novel to be called "The Story of Jurgis: A Sequel to 'The Jungle.'" If you will do this, I shall go away at once and take a much needed rest for a month or two, and I will then go out to Chicago and familiarize myself with the city's world of vice and crime, as I did with Packingtown. I will entirely rewrite the second half. . . . I will elaborate the incidents and make the characters more definite. I will work the last chapters more carefully, making them less a matter of ideas and more of persons.

Just how disappointed and aggrieved Sinclair was with the conclusion he felt he had to put in print because Brett would not accept his "definite" and "final" proposition he expressed five years later in correspondence with Gaylord Wilshire: "Think of my having had to ruin the Jungle [*sic*] with an ending so pitifully inadequate, because we were actually without money for food." Matters might have turned out even worse, however. Of his first attempt at a conclusion, he recalled,

> I ran wild at the end, attempting to solve all the problems of America; I put in the Moyer-Haywood case, everything I knew and thought my readers ought to know. I submitted these chapters to a test, and got a cruel verdict; the editor of the "Appeal" came to visit me, and sat in my little living room one evening to hear the story—and fell sound asleep.

The editor, Fred Warren, did better than that. He made Sinclair hack out a lot of the surplussage, and apparently we owe the shape of the last four chapters partially to him.

We also owe to him—or to J. A. Wayland, who owned the *Appeal*—the mysterious conclusion to one of the strangest episodes in the history of serial fiction. With the issue of November 4, 1905, the *Appeal* abruptly ceased publishing installments of *The Jungle*, at the end of what would become Chapter 28 in the book version. No explanation was offered by the editor, nor did Sinclair even mention this event in his many accounts of his most famous endeavor. One might wonder if, knowing how garbled and eccentric were the concluding chapters to come, the paper chose to suppress them. But not exactly. More tantalizing yet was the note the editor appended to the announcement, acknowledging the truncation of the narrative and offering to send the concluding episodes to any reader who sent in ten cents for them. No copy of a completely separate printing of these chapters has come to light, but they were in fact already published by the time the *Appeal* made this offer. All the while *The Jungle* had been appearing in weekly segments in the *Appeal*, it had also been appearing in much larger segments in the quarterly Socialist journal, *One Hoss Philosophy*, which was also owned by Wayland and published in Girard. The October, 1905, number included all the final chapters as Sinclair originally intended them to be published, and it may have been a copy of this which the *Appeal* proposed to supply for a curious reader's dime.

Whatever the reasons for this peculiar editorial behavior, it explains one curiosity in the responses to *The Jungle*. Jack London was one of the tale's most fervid admirers, and, just two weeks after the *Appeal*'s termination of the serial, he published in the *Appeal* a plea for readers to subscribe to a privately printed book version of the novel. London compared this new achievement to its most important predecessor in the field of American anti-capitalist fiction:

> The beautiful theoretics of Bellamy's "Looking Backward" are all very good. They served their purpose, and served it well. "Looking Backward" was a great book, but I dare say "The Jungle," which has not beautiful theoretics, is an even greater book.

In contrast with Bellamy's work, Sinclair's seemed to London "alive and warm," "brutal with life," "written of sweat and blood." But London obviously had read only what had appeared in the *Appeal*, for the concluding chapters, which were already available in *One Hoss Philosophy*, are laden with "theoretics," and singularly lacking in the gusto and guts London appreciated. Just why Sinclair betrayed his promise and London's advertisement can best be accounted for by the logic of his talent and his intentions.

Sinclair insisted that he was not writing merely a muckraking exposé or a "naturalist" novel after the fashion of Zola, but a book which would show the economic forces driving the working class to socialism. In his search for narrative closure, he was, therefore, under the constraint, which has long bedeviled radical fiction, of demonstrating just how this process might happen in the instance of the working-class characters in his narrative. His choice of the conversion motif was appropriate to the pattern of the fiction he had already established, and was in harmony with his own experience and personality. Sinclair was a man of words, inordinately confident that he could change the world with rhetoric. The embrace of socialism in Sinclair's narrative is a psychic event, not a social or economic one, and not so much rational or logical in its development as it is emotional. The sermon is the appropriate medium, pure "theoretics" the message.

Sinclair's introduction of Jurgis to socialism is, however, significantly more elaborate than the bare pattern of revelation and communication. The four chapters which London had not read *begin* with Jurgis' conversion, but reveal also the entire world of the Socialist movement in Chicago as Sinclair knew it, and examine in some detail just how Sinclair conceived a working-class recruit might fit into it.

The wedding feast, so effectively evoked in the first chapters, presented a standard of life, the folk community, against which to judge the economic and social system that, by the end of the novel, has destroyed almost all the people who dance their hearts out in that tawdry saloon. The inner world of the Socialist movement in the last chapters provides a contrasting, new, and possible standard of life, which is supposed to define the failures of the present society even more clearly and also solve the problems and dissipate the anxieties of the author, his surviving characters, and his audience. The function of these chapters is to achieve psychic balance and repose by creating in imagination the ideal future as it might actually be lived in the present. This attempt was deeply rooted in Sinclair's "theoretics" and in his private life.

Another function of these closing chapters and their "theoretics," perhaps not so intentional, is to allay the fears of the non-Socialist reader that socialism might actually threaten the American middle-class way of life. Sinclair made it quite plain that he would not impose on society the culture, manners, and character of the kind of working people the novel was written about.

The narrative of Jurgis' conversion—the representation of the psychic process of it, and the effects upon his life-style and situation—is what we finally want to consider, but the actual content of the world view and political program to which Sinclair would have working people adhere also needs scrutiny.

The explanation of the principles of socialism and the Socialist critique of capitalism in the last four chapters of *The Jungle* are developed through a number of narrative strategies, mainly rhetorical occasions. The two most important are the oration, which converts Jurgis at the end of Chapter 28, and the debate among the Socialists who gather at the home of the "man named Fisher" in the last chapter. Further, there are the lessons given by Comrade Ostrinski, the explanations Sinclair offers more or less in his own voice, and the anonymous election-night speech with which the novel ends. Each major occasion has a tone and quality of its own. In addition, Sinclair's next book, *Industrial Republic* (1907), may be referred to as a gloss upon the politics of these concluding chapters.

The oration, which is Jurgis' introduction to the Socialist movement, is an extreme example of a familiar strain on the pious and the sentimental in early Socialist though. Although the sermon goes on for many pages without much development, a passage like the following contains virtually the whole message:

> . . . if once the vision of my soul were spoken upon earth, if once the anguish of its defeat were uttered in human speech, it would break the stoutest barriers of prejudice, it would shake the most sluggish soul to action; it would abash the most cynical, it would terrify the most selfish; and the voice of mockery would be silenced, and fraud and falsehood would slink back into their dens, and the truth would stand forth alone! For I speak with the voice of the millions who are voiceless! Of them that are oppressed and have no comforter! Of the disinherited of life, for whom there is no respite and no deliverance, to whom the world is a prison, a dungeon of torture, a tomb!

As the evangelical diction insists, Sinclair's politics were pure "social gospel." The word "socialism" is not spoken by the orator who converts Jurgis. Later, when one of Jurgis' informants does use the term, it is to insist upon the quasi-religious character of this belief: Socialism "was the new religion of humanity—or you might say it was the fulfillment of the old religion, since it implied but the literal application of all the teachings of Christ." In these last chapters, Sinclair was at pains to demonstrate the various characters of the Socialist movement, and this address is presented as only *one* voice of liberation, but Sinclair indicates in several ways that this pious rhetoric is his familiar mode of discourse. Indeed, his own language is often laden with the same diction, and in the film version of *The Jungle*, which was made in 1913, Sinclair acted the part of this orator who introduced Jurgis to socialism.

The actual content of the argument at the end of *The Jungle* placed Sinclair in the right wing of American socialism in the early years of the century, but Sinclair was distinctly Marxian in many ways, advocating class conflict, and anticipating the revolutionary expropriation of industry and the take-over of government from the capitalist class. Jurgis' first evening as a Socialist ends with him restless in ecstasy over "the glory of that joyful vision of the people of Packingtown marching in and taking possession of the Union Stockyards!" The book ends with a promise and a threat: "Chicago will be ours! *Chicago will be ours!* CHICAGO WILL BE OURS!" But Sinclair's revolutionary class struggle seems relatively painless all the same.

Socialism according to Sinclair has two simple tenets:

> First . . . a Socialist leader believes in the common ownership and democratic management of the means of producing the necessities of life; and second . . . a socialist [*sic*] believes that the means by which this is to be brought about is the class-conscious political organization of the wage earner.

The emphasis is on the political. Sinclair rejected trade union organization as a means of revolutionary activity. He was no syndicalist. Jurgis has a brief fit of enthusiasm for unions (end of Chapter 8) when he discovers and joins the one in Packingtown, but (contrary to what Sinclair's original précis promised) the union plays no great part in Jurgis' life, and its only major action, the strike, is seen from the other side, with Jurgis, the hapless foreman of the scabs, barricaded inside the yards. Jurgis' Socialist mentor, Ostrinski, explains the "union organization did the workers little good, for the employers were organized also; and so the strikes generally failed, and as fast as the unions were broken up the men were coming over to the Socialists."

Sinclair could acknowledge in a perfunctory way the possibility that, if the capitalists refused to accept a freely elected Socialist government, "Why then there will be violence." But he did not enjoy the prospect, nor did he take it very seriously. He went out of his way to assure his readers that the packinghouse workers under extreme stress of a strike did not initiate violence, and that reports of violence were invented by the press. He criticized Jurgis' excessive zeal in attempting to brow-beat other workers into joining the union, "after the fashion of all crusaders since the original ones, who set out to spread the gospel of Brotherhood by force of arms." The obvious intention of the anarchist episode indicated in the original précis was to reject terrorism as a means of overthrowing capitalism.

The Jungle ends with statistical glee, tallying the vote and celebrating the significant gains of the Socialist party in the elections of 1904. We get a long list of the most impressive jumps of voting strength—especially in Chicago. "Thus Chicago now led the country; it had set a new standard for the party, it had shown the workingmen the way!" *The* way.

It should be observed that such an optimistic assessment of the chances of gaining socialism through the ballot rather than the bullet had a certain impetus in the facts at hand. The recent history of Socialist electoral politics in western Europe and the United States seemed encouraging. The Socialist vote in Chicago had multiplied seven times in four years. But Sinclair's optimism was particularly shallow. In *Industrial Republic* he acknowledged the anxieties of his presumed audience. "Revolution" is a word with "an ominous sound." "The reader thinks of street battles and barricades." "By a Revolution," Sinclair said, "I mean the complete transfer of the economic and political power of the country from the hands of the present exploiting class to the hands of the whole people." That presumably sounds less ominous, especially when we find out why and how it is probably going to be painless:

> . . . in the accomplishment of this purpose the people will proceed, as in everything else they do, along the line of least resistance. It is very much less trouble to cast a ballot than it is to go out in the streets and shoot; and our people are used to the ballot method.

The singular achievement of this intriguing vision of revolutionary triumph is Sinclair's prediction that the process would prove successful by the year 1913, shortly after the election to the presidency, on the Democratic ticket, of William Randolph Hearst.

There are a number of other things remarkable about Sinclair's political opinions. Although he did not shy from the idea of class conflict, and did not propose a reconciliation of capitalists and workers in the Cooperative Commonwealth, he argued that the revolution will mean transfer of power from the capitalist class—not to the working class but to "the whole people," which is a formulation out of liberal democracy, not out of Marx. Oddly he doesn't even consider the Socialist party as the agency through which power is to be assumed. The party is not a triumphant vanguard, but only a threat and pressure from the rear, thus:

> The Socialist party is a party of agitation rather than administration; but it is of vital importance that it should everywhere exist, as a party of the last resort, a club held over Society. Everywhere the cry will be: Do this, and do that, or the Socialists will carry the country.

A non-Socialist government under a "radical Democrat"—like Hearst—will be induced by this "club" to invent socialism in spite of itself by taking over the industries which have collapsed during the next economic crisis (due about 1912).

Of the coming revolution, Sinclair explained lightheartedly that "it is a charmingly simple process—I could do it all myself":

> . . . it is only safe to say that there will be as little change as possible in the business methods of the country—and so little that the man who should come back and look at it from the outside, would not even know that any change had taken place.

The only difference will be that the industries will run more efficiently and the workers will get the profits, and this increased efficiency and income will free people to enjoy "the life of the spirit." This is the "new religion of humanity" Sinclair would have a humble Lithuanian working stiff receive into his heart.

The last chapters of *The Jungle* seem "tacked on" for two reasons. The more obvious, and the one usually commented on, is the difficulty of crediting Jurgis' conversion. It is psychologically unconvincing, and seems to serve only the demand of Sinclair's didactic purpose. The other reason is that these chapters begin a new and qualitatively different kind of narrative—a new story, a new type of character, a new world. Having spent most of the book on Jurgis' turf, Sinclair concluded by introducing Jurgis to the circle in which Sinclair himself lived and was comfortable. The working-class character Sinclair bases his narrative on is neither heroic nor pathetic, but is rather like L'il Abner most of the time: innocent, good-hearted, strong, gullible, forever doing what he is told by an outrageous variety of masters. He seldom acts in defiance, and, when he does take initiative, it is usually within the framework of what his domestic responsibilities dictate. (It is significant, I think, that the only other working-class "hero" in Sinclair's fiction was the perennial drudge-worker of social movements, the perplexed, willing, humbled grunt, Jimmie Higgins.)

Jurgis' psychic life is elementary, to say the least. Domestic happiness and domestic responsibility are the goal and burden of his thought, and, after he is ravished of the one and freed from the other, he is haunted by the memory of the enjoyment of the tender familial emotions—either haunted, or debauching himself in forgetfulness. His manhood is tied to his faithful dedication to the domestic sentiments. His degradation is equivalent to loss of consciousness of family life and its joys.

In such a degraded state of mind, Jurgis receives socialism. The experience is energetically, if not profoundly, religious, and the psychic chaos of it is strong in force and fever. Jurgis' first awareness at the meeting into which he has crawled for a few hours' warmth is not of the Socialist orator's words, but of their effect upon the "lady" who sits next to him. The intensity of the description is sexually distressing and almost pathological:

> There was a look of excitement upon her face, of tense effort, as of one struggling mightily, or witnessing a struggle. There was a faint quivering of her nostrils; and now and then she would moisten her lips with feverish haste. Her bosom rose and fell as she breathed, and her excitement seemed to mount higher and higher, and then sink away again, like a boat tossing upon ocean surges.

Jurgis cannot figure our what is going on, and works himself into a state of extreme psychic disorder:

> It was like coming suddenly upon some wild sight of nature—a mountain forest lashed by a tempest, a ship tossed about upon a stormy sea. Jurgis had an unpleasant sensation, a sense of confusion, of disorder, of wild and meaningless uproar.

Into this consciousness, the orator's message beings to penetrate. Sinclair breaks into the oration once to indicate the progress of Jurgis' mind: "he was trembling, smitten with wonder." ("Wonder" is the same feeling that the immigrants had in response to all the new noxious fumes and ingenious machines that Sinclair introduced them to early in the novel.) By the conclusion of the sermon, Jurgis has been saved. He has been put back in touch with his manhood—that is, with his capacity for sentiment: "a flood of emotion surged up in him—all his old hopes and longings, his old griefs and rages and despairs."

The orator's appeal to pity for the suffering poor—the women driven to prostitution, the children to starvation, the men to death—and the religious conception and rhetoric of the argument are perfectly suited to appeal to the kind of rudimentary consciousness Sinclair attributed to Jurgis. What sways Jurgis is hardly the bright light of what Sinclair on other occasions, was pleased to call "Scientific Socialism." Rather, it is quite the opposite of rational understanding. The orator's voice "shook him and startled him with sudden fright, with a sense of things not of earth, of mysteries never spoken before, of presences of awe and terror!" The orator seems to Jurgis a "miraculous man," a "master wizard." Jurgis, who has supposedly been made a man again, turns out to have been made a beast. He jumps from his chair "with his clenched hands upraised, his eyes bloodshot, and the veins standing out purple in his face, roaring in the voice of a wild beast, frantic, incoherent, maniacal."

What was Sinclair's intention? Certainly he must have believed that this whole embarrassing episode was doing what everything else in the book was meant to do: convince the reader of the necessity for and validity of socialism. One knows that such stark and frantic and intense experiences of conversion do occur, and one might assume that there is something of Sinclair's own experience in the fiction. But the effect of this passage in Jurgis' life, like most of those that will follow it, is to prevent the reader from taking Jurgis seriously as a man and as a Socialist.

Here, he is bestial and hysterical. Yet, he is also shown to be drab, timid, and complacently inferior. Comrade Ostrinski says when he takes Jurgis in tow after the meeting: "We will make a fighter out of you!" But Ostrinski's promise is not kept. One the one occasion on which Jurgis does *anything* in his role as an active member of the Socialist party, he seems little better than a buffoon. The Socialists plan to pack a Democratic Party campaign rally:

> Jurgis, who had insisted upon coming, had the time of his life that night; he danced about and waved his arms in his excite-ment—and at the very climax he broke loose from his friends, and got out into the aisle, and proceeded to make a speech himself.

Jurgis seems a mindless character whom his friends, in his wild moments, need to restrain.

The extent to which Sinclair demeans and hobbles Jurgis is remark-able. Jurgis gets a job in a hotel which turns out to be owned by a Socialist, one Tommy Hinds. Employer and employee are delighted to discover they are comrades: "So, after that, Jurgis was know to his 'boss' as 'Comrade Jurgis,' and in return he was expected to call him 'Comrade Hinds'." Even among Socialists in Sinclair's ken, employees are "expected" to keep their place, defer to their betters, and like their menial jobs. Jurgis' work is scrub-bing spittoons and polishing banisters, "and to keep Hinds' hotel a thing of beauty was his joy in life." Sinclair offers the most banal apology for Jurgis' lowly station: "His outward life was commonplace and uninteresting; he was just a hotel porter, and expected to remain one while he lived; but meantime, in the realm of thought, his life was a perpetual adventure."

In the last chapter, in final ignominy and social insignificance, Jurgis virtually disappears from the novel, swallowed up in the parlor debate of the Socialist intelligentsia. He is taken to visit the place of the "man named Fisher, a Chicago millionaire who had given up his life to settlement work, and had a little home in the heart of the city's slums," a character probably suggested by George D. Herron and Gaylord Wilshire, wealthy radicals whom Sinclair had recently come to know. The occasion is created to expose "the editor of a big Eastern magazine, who wrote against Socialism," to the arguments of the Socialists. It is a marvelous affair, as befits the "little home" of a kindhearted millionaire, who, like his editor guest, is appropriately "clad in evening dress." More uncomfortable for Jurgis is the discovery that three of the guests are "ladies." "He had never talked to people of this sort before, and he fell into an agony of embarrassment. He stood in the doorway clutching his hat tightly in his hands, and made a deep bow to each of the persons as he was introduced." Although he had been invited as an expert on the crimes of the meat packers, "he was terrified lest they should expect him to talk." He is *not* asked to talk. He is mentioned only once more in the novel at the end of the ensuing debate, when he notices, without consequences, a pretty young woman, and is said to think, without acting, that it would be nice to speak with her.

Jurgis merely evaporates. Sinclair could not hang his conclusion on the character he has manipulated throughout the novel. That character, because of his social, cultural, and economic background, does not fit into the polite society of the Socialist movement, so Sinclair dropped him.

The grip of such class distinctions upon the imagination of early Socialist writers in the United States is confirmed by the fictional strategies of Jack London, who faced the same problem Sinclair did during the same period: How to create a working-class hero? London took the other way out, and, most prominently in *Martin Eden* (1907) and *The Iron Heel* (1908), turned his ill-couth protagonists into proper gentlemen, capable of mastering the daughters of wealth and culture. It is easy to trace in the lives and characters of Sinclair and London reasons for their contrary solutions to this literary problem. The point is to appreciate how acute a problem it was, and how the more-or-less Marxian political beliefs they brought to their fiction forced them to extreme solutions.

In spite of the unprecedented candor and empathy with which Sinclair was able to treat immigrant working-class life at crucial points of his narrative, the startling final diminution of Jurgis' character and role is not one for which we have been unprepared. In the anonymous oratory that converts Jurgis, Sinclair articulated his own contradictions. The orator affirms Sinclair's own assertion of identity with the poor: "I know, for I have been in your place, I have lived your life, and there is no man before me here to-night who knows it better." But the orator goes out of his way to insist that he is morally and intellectually (and, by implication, socially) superior to his audience: "I am not surprised that I find you sordid and material, sluggish and incredulous." Capitalism, he argues, is to be overcome in part "by the painful gropings of the untutored mind, by the feeble stammerings of the uncultured voice."

At his worst, Sinclair could shift from condescension to contempt—even to vulgar racist and national chauvinist contumely of the working class. True, the passage I have in mind characterizes strike-breakers, "scabs," who are helping the packers to defy the honest union workers. But these are the same kind of people, socially and ethnically, who are out on strike, and the net effect of this characterization is not so much to enlighten the working-class reader about the depravity of scabbing as it is to reinforce the polite reader's stock attitudes toward "inferior" peoples, and to appeal gratuitously to the white reader's racism:

> As very few of the better class of workmen could be got for such work [strike-breaking], these specimens of the New American hero contained an assortment of the criminals and thugs of the city, besides negroes and the lowest foreigners—Greeks, Roumanians, Sicilians, and Slovaks. They have been attracted more by the prospect of disorder than by the big wages; and they made the night hideous with singing and carousing, and only went to sleep when the time came for them to get up to work.

The parallels between this situation and the situation with which the book begins are striking. The chaotic late-night noise and drinking of the foreigners at the wedding feast are represented in such a way as to contradict the stock response of the respectable observer. Here, on the contrary, Sinclair called upon those same conventional attitudes, as it suited his convenience. Note that Sinclair did not mention Lithuanians among the "lowest foreigners." Earlier he had observed that the Slovaks were "lower" than the Lithuanians in the social order of Packingtown—that is to say, more recently arrived and more exploited. But here the clear suggestion is that they are "low" in character, in the same sense as "criminals and thugs." Still, nothing in the book gives any basis, much less justification, for discriminating between Lithuanians and other "inferior" people of Europe.

Sinclair was most offensive in his characterization of black laborers. Jurgis, working as a scab foreman, discovers in his charge "a throng of stupid black negroes" who do not want to work, who steal knives to cut each other up with, who create chaos on the killing beds, and are insolent, to boot: "'See hyar, boss,' a big, black 'buck' would begin, 'ef you doan' like de way Ah does dis job, you kin get somebody else to do it!'" Sinclair reaffirmed every notion and fear in the repertoire of racism, and especially the vision of brute sexual threat to white womanhood. In a throng attending a prizefight in the strike-bound yards, Sinclair saw

> . . . young white girls from the country rubbing elbows with big buck negroes with daggers in their boots, while rows of woolly heads peered down from every window of the surrounding facto-ries. The ancestors of these black people had been savages in Africa; and since then they had been chattel slaves, or had been held down by a community ruled by traditions of slavery. Now for the first time they were free—free to gratify every passion, free to wreck themselves. . . .

> [The packers] lodged men and women on the same floor; and with the night there began a saturnalia of debauchery—scenes such as never before had been witnessed in America. And as the women were the dregs from the brothels of Chicago, and the men were for the most part of ignorant country negroes, the nameless diseases of vice were soon rife; and this where food was being handled which was sent out to every corner of the civilized world.

Clearly Sinclair did not "accidentally" hit his reader's stomach; he aimed straight at it!

The contrast between the working world of the yards and the little world of the Chicago Socialist movement in the closing chapters of *The Jungle* is stark. The bosom of socialism is a comfortable place where, among other characters, women are ladies, and gentlemen wear evening dress. There *are* other characters. There is Tommy Hinds, who uses the lobby of his cozy hotel for a schoolroom. There are great men like Eugene Debs and Jack London (described without being named), who come through Chicago on speaking tours. And there are the two cranks to whom Sinclair gives the penultimate episode of the novel, Comrade Schliemann, the Swedish food faddist, ex-professor, and militant atheist, and Comrade Lucas, the former Protestant minister, who argues that Jesus was the founder of the Socialist movement. To these cordial opponents Sinclair gave the task of outlining his own views about the future of socialism, how efficiently the farms will be run, how drink and hairdressers will be abandoned, and how the whole meat-packing industry will finally shut down when people become "refined" enough to give up eating meat altogether. What Sinclair was apparently trying to demonstrate is that the Socialist movement is intellectually heterogeneous and tolerant of internal debate—is, and always will be: "'Communism in material production, anarchism in intellectual' was the formula of modern proletarian thought." Sinclair had his debators explain at some length how writers and artists and philosophers would have complete freedom to compete in the marketplace of the Cooperative Commonwealth. In other words, Sinclair, who had spent a whole book immersed in the lives of laboring people, was ultimately most interested in the intelligentsia and its problems. A Socialist was, for him, someone who could make or write an argument. The Socialist party was an agitprop group, and socialism would come by eloquent persuasion.

In his *Autobiography*, Sinclair explains that before he became a Socialist he was "intellectually a perfect little snob and tory": "I expected social evils to be remedied by culture and well-mannered gentlemen who had been to college and acquired noble ideas." The concluding chapters of *The Jungle* do not indicate that he had really changed his mind very much. He did, however, continue to change those chapters.

The last section of the original published text of *The Jungle* (which appeared only in *One Hoss Philosophy*), treating of Jurgis' discovery of socialism and its aftermath, differs substantially from the corresponding last four chapters as published the following year by Doubleday, Page, after Macmillian and five other commercial houses had turned it down. In addition to rearranging his chapter divisions, so that the original thirty-six sorted out into thirty-two, Sinclair edited his text to shrink (and garble) a penultimate episode, and to lop off his original concluding event altogether.

The political rally in the stockyards at which Jurgis had "the time of his life" and seemed to act so foolishly is described in much greater detail, and his impulsive speech is produced rather than just mentioned. This once, Sinclair allowed Jurgis to speak somewhat like a recent immigrant, with an accent: "'I lived here in de stockyards once!' he cried—'I helped sell out de people! I have known Tom Cassidy! Every god damned cent dat feller got he git from de packers.'" Much more important, Sinclair explained the motivation behind what seemed, in the subsequent book version, Jurgis' odd behavior at the meeting. One is reminded that Jurgis had jumped bail to escape being jailed for assaulting (a second time) the foreman who had seduced Ona. Returning to the stockyards to attend this political rally was, therefore, foolish. Sure enough, the foreman spots Jurgis, who is arrested once again on the old charge.

Sinclair had to drop Jurgis' arrest, because he deleted its consequence, the last paragraph of the story as originally published. The book version ends with the triumphant Socialist election victory speech: "CHICAGO WILL BE OURS!" The *One Hoss Philosophy* version carried a few more lines:

> All of which was at one o'clock on the morning of the day after the election; and at one o'clock of the afternoon of the same day Jurgis was handcuffed to a detective, and on his way to serve a two years' sentence in state's prison for assault with intent to kill.

Thus, the progress of Sinclair's search for a way to conclude an "*Uncle Tom's Cabin* of Wage Slavery" led away from engagement with (even sympathy for) working class life, and away from a potentially interesting complex vision of the interrelations between historic process and the fate of individuals. He suppressed a conclusion that sharply contrasted generalized political optimism with the unremitting victimization of Jurgis, for whom, as an individual, socialism does not offer exemption. The end of the Doubleday, Page version is much more simplistic. The deletion of Jurgis' last hardship also reduces to naught his role—the worker's role—in the political climax of the fiction.

Nor was Sinclair yet through tampering with his conclusion. (This last is a footnote to a peculiar tale, but an indicative one.) Hardly was *The Jungle* out in book form before he arranged for a dramatization of the story, hoping for another big hit, a wider audience, and more royalties. The actual responsibility for the reworking of the plot fell to a person named Margaret Mayo, who was the wife of a play broker, Edgar Selwyn, but Sinclair gave his imprimatur to her version of the plot, and was intimately enough involved in the project to be reliably suspected of an adulterous relation with his collaborator.

In this retelling, much of the sensational material about life in the stockyards from the first half of the novel is retained, as much as could fit upon a stage. The plot gains its crisis in the assault upon Ona's virtue and Jurgis' imprisonment. They do lose a child, but Ona does not die in childbirth. The final scene combines the politics of the last four chapters into a single event—a political rally in a saloon into which Jurgis wanders during his search for his displaced family after his release from prison. There he discovers not only socialism but also his lost wife: "The two remain in each others' arms. Meeting breaks up in general confusion as—CURTAIN FALLS."

In one last capitulation, Sinclair authorized (if he did not himself write) a drastic shift of his plot to suit the conventions of the commercial stage, and turned a tragedy of working-class life, the premier work of "proletarian literature" in America, into a domestic comedy.

MORRIS DICKSTEIN

Introduction to The Jungle

Very few works of literature have actually changed the course of history, and critics have usually been suspicious of those that did. Compared to propaganda, literature usually influences life in subtle and indirect ways. It can alter our sense of reality and affect the climate of opinion; but books that create sensational controversies may well sacrifice the deeper purposes of literature to immediate effect, and they often appeal cheaply to the reader's emotions. Upton Sinclair's *The Jungle*, first published serially in 1905 and in book form in 1906, has an unshakable reputation as just such a work. It is remembered as a stomach-turning exposé of unsanitary conditions and deceitful practices in the meat-packing industry; as such it aroused the ire of a whole nation, from President Theodore Roosevelt on down, and it contributed enormously to the landmark passage of the Pure Food and Drug Act of 1906. (The book is said to have decreased America's meat consumption for decades.)

Though *The Jungle* is still very widely read, in part as a historical document, few critics take the book or its author seriously anymore. Like *Uncle Tom's Cabin*, to which it has often been compared, *The Jungle* is considered agitation rather than art; its blunt, naturalistic method, surfeited with sickening details, is considered crude even in comparison to the writing of Sinclair's immediate predecessors, unflinching realists like Theodore

From *The Jungle* by Upton Sinclair. Introduction © 1981 by Bantam Books.

Dreiser, Frank Norris, and Stephen Crane. These men went down in literary history as important novelists, even when their technique had gone out of fashion. Sinclair went down in history as a muckraker, a talented progressive journalist and reformer with no literary technique whatsoever.

This firmly held picture needs serious revision, for it can't stand up to a careful examination of the book itself and it doesn't help us understand Sinclair's long and tumultuous career as a writer, agitator, and occasional political candidate. Sinclair himself always insisted that people had misread *The Jungle:* he had intended it less as an exposé of the meat industry than as an argument for socialism, to which he had recently been converted. ("I aimed at the public's heart, and by accident I hit it in the stomach.") For this misunderstanding he had only himself to blame, for the book had made him a famous public figure overnight, and he cunningly played on its notoriety with all the wiles of a born publicist. Attacked by the big meat packers, he peppered the country with articles and statements supporting the details of his novel, nearly all of which were soon confirmed by independent investigation. Invited down to the White House by Teddy Roosevelt, he followed up his visit with a barrage of letters that left the president exasperated.

Though he sometimes fell for cranky and faddish ideas, such as fasting cures and mental telepathy, the irrepressible Sinclair continued to play this gadfly role for decades. He became something of an American institution, a one-man reform movement and radical crusader—a part quite out of keeping with everything in his earlier life. Sinclair was born in Baltimore in 1878, just two years before another hometown troublemaker-to-be, H. L. Mencken. His parents were impoverished Southern gentry, and his father's Virginia ancestry included longtime Naval traditions and catastrophic Confederate loyalties. They moved to New York when Upton was eight or nine and lived in a succession of cheap rooming houses, as his father slowly destroyed himself with drink and his mother, acutely feeling her decline in status, gave Upton heavy doses of religion and morality. A phenomenal reader with a quick, retentive memory, the boy had no formal schooling until the age of eleven; but by fourteen he had entered New York's City College and soon afterwards began to moonlight as a writer of jokes and pulp fiction. Before turning to serious writing he churned out a staggering quantity of juvenile potboilers, working with a fluency and prodigious energy that never abandoned him.

By 1900 Sinclair had vowed to make his mark as an artist. He wrote several romantic and subjective novels, which got little attention and left him desperately poor. The turning point in his life came when he joined the Socialist Party in 1904, quickly becoming one of its most vocal campaigners for social and economic reform. After it was founded, in 1901, the party enjoyed more than a decade of extraordinary growth, which climaxed in the excellent showing of its candidate, Eugene V. Debs, in the presidential election of 1912. "Starting with 10,000 members in 1901," says historian James Weinstein, "The Party had grown to 118,000 by 1912, had elected some 1,200 public officials throughout the United States, and was publishing over 300 periodicals of all kinds." This Socialist upsurge primarily took place not in the urban ghettoes of the East, under the influence of European ideologies, but in the vast American heartland, then undergoing the strains of industrialization. A great deal of rural populist strength fed into this Socialist tide. The deepest inroads were in states like Oklahoma, which later became bulwarks of conservatism. Mayors were elected in towns like Schenectady (New York), Butte (Montana), Granite City (Illinois), Davenport (Iowa), Lackawanna (New York), Berkeley (California), New Castle (Pennsylvania), and Flint (Michigan)—most often, as Weinstein notes, "in small or medium-sized railroad, mining, or industrial centers." (The most powerful American journalist of the twentieth century, Walter Lippmann, began his career in 1991 as secretary to Socialist Mayor Lunn of Schenectady.)

Close to the center of all this Socialist activity was a rambunctious and spectacularly successful weekly newspaper out of Girard, Kansas, called *Appeal to Reason*, which cost subscribers twenty-five cents a year and was written in the breezy muckraking style of Midwestern populism. In line with so much of the native American socialism that preceded the Russian Revolution, the paper avoided ideological factions and sectarian dogmatism. Like the Marxism of Upton Sinclair—for he was formed by this prewar climate—the socialism of the *Appeal* was less a science of history than a compound of moral indignation, quasi-religious fervor, and a set of simple truths about the social and economic system. The paper had a passion for social justice, the rights of labor, and the exposure of corruption. This formula, which was not far from folk wisdom, proved amazingly popular. Late in 1904, when the editor sent Sinclair to Chicago to examine conditions in the stockyards, the *Appeal*'s circulation was over half a million and heading upwards. The resulting novel, based on seven weeks of intensive research, was serialized in the *Appeal* and achieved great notoriety even before it came out as a book.

Chicago in the summer of 1904 had been the scene of an unsuccessful strike against the huge meat-packing companies, the so-called Beef Trust. What attracted Sinclair was the raw industrial climate of the city, not the problem of adulterated meat. He signed on with the *Appeal* to tell the story of workingmen and women subjugated and finally ground under by vast monopolistic enterprises. But once there he found that the product itself was as poorly regulated as the horrible conditions under which it was produced, that labor and consumer interests were identical and one could be used to draw graphic attention to the other. He discovered that the way to the public's heart was through its stomach, and thus he inadvertently became one of the fathers of the consumer protection movement. Whatever nostalgia we may have for deregulation can scarcely survive Sinclair's portrait of laissez-faire industrial capitalism in its buccaneering phase. But his device was so effective, the picture he painted was so gruesome and unforgettable, that it obscured his original intention. Sinclair spiced his sociology with bits and pieces of a horror-film scenario, and though it occupies relatively few pages, this was the putrid taste that people remembered.

The ultimate importance of *The Jungle* lies elsewhere. From the epic poems of Homer to the great novels of the nineteenth century, it's surprising how little literature of history is written "from below," from the point of view of the weak and dispossessed classes. Before the French Revolution—in Shakespeare, for example—servants, artisans, and peasants were usually portrayed without real dignity: as loyal retainers at best, or clownish rustics who were nimble figures of fun. The vaunted traditions of Western humanism rarely stooped to explore the inner humanity of those trapped by birth or occupation near the bottom of the social hierarchy. Even nineteenth-century novels that deal with revolutionary ferment, such as Flaubert's *Sentimental Education*, tend to individualize only middle-class characters, while treating the common people as society itself treats them, as an undifferentiated mass, a volatile, incendiary crowd or mob.

No doubt there were melodramatic explorations of the urban underworld by writers like Victor Hugo, Charles Dickens, and Eugène Sue. The industrial novels of mid-Victorian England, like Dickens's *Hard Times*, were a significant breakthrough but they often gave vague and idealized portraits of working-class characters. There were other precedents for what Sinclair was trying to do, including Zola's great novel about French miners, *Germinal*, and fellow Socialist Jack London's depiction of poverty in London's East End, *The People of the Abyss*. But Sinclair set out to propel "the workingmen of America," to whom he dedicated the book, into the center of the national consciousness. He aimed not merely to commiserate with them or to describe the conditions in which they worked but to call into question the basis of the system: the ethic of competitive individualism, which turned the urban landscape into a savage place, a jungle.

This theme sounds almost too heavy for any novel, but only in the last four chapters does it threaten to turn *The Jungle* into a tract. The first two-thirds of the book are far more concrete and vivid. *The Jungle* is a protest novel, an exposure of intolerable working and living conditions in the city of Chicago at the turn of the century. But unlike most protest novelists, who push a thesis at the expense of a credible plot and lifelike characters, Sinclair is a natural storyteller. He commands a prose so readable and transparent that it offers little resistance to translators; this has helped make him one of America's most widely read authors abroad, where America is seen as a land of opportunity but also of unbridled economic savagery.

Sinclair's other great gift is his sense of fact. In his research and interviews he was able to accumulate masses of clear information not only on the workplace and living conditions but also about machinery, transportation, profit margins, sewage, hygiene, prisons, hospitals, the courts, the political clubs—all the institutions needed to keep a modern city running. He shows not only how the meat industry and the steel industry operate but also how the machinery of power is greased, how the system of graft and patronage functions, how the bosses, the politicians, the contractors, the criminals, the magistrates, and the police work hand in glove.

Sinclair's method is too journalistic to make *The Jungle* a great city novel, but it is a very good one. From early on we notice that he is too willing to suspend his story while he takes his characters (and us) on a Cook's tour of the meat-packing plant before they actually go to work. Later he contrives to get his hero, Jurgis Rudkus, a Lithuanian immigrant trying to support a large family, into every sort of job and every corner of Chicago life. By the end Jurgis has been drawn out into a pale Everyman, a transparent device to show us how more and more of this society functions. After losing his job with the packers Jurgis spends time in court, in jail, in the harvester works, in the steel works, as a hobo on the road, as a campaign worker, a union activist, a scab, a petty criminal, a beggar, a guest in the home of the big boss's son, a hotel porter, and finally a converted socialist who has found all the right answers. The last third of the book has much less credibility than the terrible scenes that preceded it, largely because the central figure has been stretched too far. Once *The Jungle* leaves the stockyards it loses some of its grim intensity, which few novels could have managed to sustain.

Sinclair portrays the lower echelons of the industrial world as the scene of a naked struggle for survival, where workers not only are forced to compete with each other but, if they falter, are hard-pressed to keep starvation from their door and a roof over their heads. With the unions weak and cheap labor plentiful, a social Darwinist state of nature exists, a Hobbesian war of each against all. (Apologists for laissez-faire capitalism made facile use of Darwin's notion of "the survival of the fittest," as if society could be seen as a mere reflection of the state of nature.) In the hierarchy of Durham's packing plant, "all the men of the same rank were pitted against each other; the accounts of each were kept separately, and every man lived in terror of losing his job, if another made a better record than he. So from top to bottom the place was simply a seething cauldron of jealousies and hatreds."

When Jurgis is in bed with his first serious injury he is compared to "Prometheus bound," to the helpless Greek Titan who first brought fire and technology to mankind, only to be deprived of his freedom. He is tormented by the idea that "he and all those who were dear to him might lie and perish of starvation and cold . . . that here in this huge city, with its heaped-up wealth, human creatures might be hunted down and destroyed by the wild-beast powers of nature, just as truly as ever they were in the days of the cave men!"

To convey this desperate vulnerability and isolation—which has slipped from our memories since the coming of the welfare state—Sinclair centers on an immigrant family whose economic problems are compounded by cultural dislocation. *The Jungle* beings with a powerful set-piece, a traditional Lithuanian wedding feast for Jurgis and his sixteen-year-old bride Ona, which they can hardly afford, and which serves as a backdrop for the tremendous changes they have already begun to encounter in the new world. Sinclair shows how capitalism creates disintegrating pressures that undermine family life, cultural ties, and moral values, despite the system's professed adherence to these traditions. Middle-class economics gives the lie to middle-class morality. With "literally not a month's wages between them and starvation," workingmen are under pressure to abandon their families, and women must sometimes choose between starvation and prostitution. Children must go out to work or to beg before they get much schooling, and once out of the house they quickly pick up the habits of the street and the values of the new society.

Immigrants with peasant backgrounds, and even migrants from America's own rural regions, are especially ill-equipped to survive in the urban jungle because of their stubborn individualism. Jurgis relies on his own strong back to carry his family, to cope with inhuman work; but he simply becomes a cog in the industrial machine, to be discarded as soon as he shows signs of wear. Jurgis and his family are desperate to own something, to be on their own; scarcely knowing the language, they are easily swindled when they put everything they have into buying a small house. Sinclair pays little attention to the kinds of support systems that were often available as safety nets for ethnic groups: mutual aid societies, religious institutions, credit unions, relief agencies. By painting the picture in stark colors he is trying to demonstrate, as Steinbeck would later do with his Okie family in *The Grapes of Wrath*, that peasant individualism is helpless before the new juggernauts of corporate power. He shows that isolation and self-reliance are formulas for weakness and self-destruction; only the solidarity of unions can give workers economic strength.

Though conditions were harsh for workingmen then, one of the flaws of the novel is that Sinclair stacks the deck. Once things begin going bad for

Jurgis, *everything* goes bad: there is a touch of the soap opera in this succession of tragedies. As in the fate-haunted novels of Thomas Hardy, the author cannot resist putting his finger on the scales, so that the plot conforms to his own pessimism. Worse still, as soon as Jurgis discovers socialism, everything goes magically right for him; he seems to be living in a different universe. Part of Sinclair's problem is inherent in the naturalist novel, with its deterministic outlook and its emphasis on the manipulation of individuals by larger social and biological forces. The great naturalists like Zola and Dreiser fortunately did not adhere too closely to their own pseudoscientific ideas. They recognized that novelistic characters cannot begin to exist without a modicum of freedom; they must have some capacity to surprise us, to reshuffle their lives, to say and do things that seem arbitrary and unexpected.

Sinclair's characters are conceived in more constricted terms, without condescension but without much human dimension. Again and again the omniscient author sees them "like rats in a trap," stalked by "fate" or riveted to their own "destiny," little more than "cogs in the great packing machine." Though the characters' lives are rich in circumstantial detail, they can never quite bear the burden of all Sinclair wants their experiences to say. When the veil begins to fall from their eyes, when they see what their lives are really like, we feel the author behind them pulling the strings, giving Jurgis all his own understanding of the economic system. Jurgis does not have enough inner life to make his final conversion credible. Even in its powerful early chapters, the book demands a surprisingly narrow range of emotion from the reader. The more the characters are trapped by the system, they are transformed from agents to mere victims, and the principal feeling asked of us is pity—one of the most dehumanizing of all emotions, since it turns people into objects of our compassion rather than subjects in their own right.

This somewhat stunted humanity prevents *The Jungle* from being one of the truly great novels of city life, however accurate its social and economic framework may be. The Chicago of *The Jungle* is a Chicago limned by a brilliantly articulate and observant journalist, who can lay bare all the gears of the machine and show where all the people fit in. The Chicago of Dreiser's *Sister Carrie*, on the other hand, published just a few years earlier, is not just a social and economic system but, like Balzac's Paris, a Roman arena of will and desire, a field of hopes and possibilities entirely outside the range of Sinclair's characters.

Dreiser's characters, too, are limited creatures, mercilessly observed from a considerable distance by the author. Their plans often go awry, but they are never simply victims suffering against an urban backdrop; the city helps create their needs, fill out their minds, feed their hopes. Newly arrived from a small town, unable to find work, Carrie is poor as a church-mouse; but the finery she sees on people in the streets and in the shop windows inflames her with thoughts she could never have had back home. Walking through one of the new department stores, she sees "nothing which she could not have used—nothing which she did not long to own." Elbowed aside by women who can afford these things, she gets her first lesson in the reality of class. She looks down at her own clothes and realizes at once how much they reveal about her, how much they define and limit her. "A flame of envy lighted in her heart. She realized in a dim way how much the city held—wealth, fashion, ease—every adornment for women, and she longed for dress and beauty with a whole heart." Dressier shows how class, identity, and personal passion are intermeshed. Writing about the department store itself, he notes that "these vast retail combinations . . . form an interesting chapter in the commercial history of our nation," but he interweaves his economic history with a tangled web of human desires. City life conditions his characters' sense of reality.

The defining thing about Sinclair's people is that no such wishes can cross their minds. Frugal immigrants, they have no frivolous moments. They live too close to the edge of survival, ghettoed in Packingtown, cut off by language as well as by poverty, sacrificed to the industrial Moloch that dominates their existence. When they find sex they get no pleasure from it, and liquor gives them only the stupor of oblivion. "Four or five miles to the east of them lay the blue waters of Lake Michigan, but for all the good it did them it might have been as far away as the Pacific Ocean. They had only Sundays, and then they were too tired to walk. They were tied to the great packing machine, and tied to it for life." The machine that maims them physically also maims their humanity. But the novelist himself, sounding the clang of destiny for his characters, contributes to this amputation and enforces what he pities. There is an accurate touch in what Sinclair describes: a life of grinding poverty in an urban ghetto is indeed cut off from the broader flow of city life—its parameters are narrow, its demands merciless. But it should include unpredictable and even joyous moments, which Sinclair's picture leaves out. His characters, like religious martyrs, relate to their environment only as exemplary sufferers, never as autonomous agents.

Sinclair's point is precisely that people who are "wage slaves" are *not* autonomous, any more than black slaves had freedom before the Civil War. From very early in the novel he compares his characters to the animals who are penned up and slaughtered every day in the stockyards, who are moved along on conveyor belts by machinery that cares nothing for their individual desires. In the monotonous killing of each of the hogs in Chapter Three ("as if his wishes, his feelings, had simply no existence at all"), Sinclair finds his key metaphor for the condition of the workingmen; a cold, efficient machinery assimilates them, a blind "Fate" swallows them up. A few of the men are even swallowed up literally when they fall into huge vats and emerge as "Durham's Pure Leaf Lard." (This was one of the few details in *The Jungle* that could not be independently confirmed when the book appeared.)

By and large it is the endless deadpan flow of concrete details, not the garish organizing metaphors, that give the book its monolithic power. Sinclair shows precisely how wounded, diseased, and pregnant animals are turned into food under just the same unhealthy conditions that soon leave healthy men wounded and diseased: "There was no heat upon the killing beds; the men might exactly as well have worked out of doors all winter. . . . On the killing beds you were apt to be covered with blood, and it would freeze solid; if you leaned against a pillar, you would freeze to that, and if you put your hand upon the blade of your knife, you would run a chance of leaving your skin on it." Grotesque injuries were inevitable, injuries for which the company would rarely take responsibility. While a man was laid up his family could starve or freeze to death, and after a series of such injuries, if he survived, he would be too crippled to go on doing the work. When Jurgis is healthy and overflowing with life he gets a job immediately; when he becomes an empty husk of his former self he is reduced to beggary. And even among beggars he finds a jungle of savage competition, in which the truly needy are often at a disadvantage.

What enabled Sinclair's novel to have its sensational impact was his enormous dossier of irrefutable detail, straightforwardly presented and linked to an affecting human drama. Very few novels convey as much sheer information as *The Jungle*—information about the food the country was eating (which attracted most of the attention), but also information about the modern work process, about how the city functioned, with its complex mesh of graft and corruption, about the poverty and degradations of its slums, and, especially in its opening chapters, about the traumatic adjustment of recent immigrants to urban American conditions. If Sinclair himself had been a foreign-born writer, his book would quickly have been acknowledged as a pioneering treatment of the immigrant experience, several decades before this became a fashionable literary theme.

Sinclair was one of the first native writers to deal with ethnic themes without condescension or disgust—with a sympathetic tolerance that unfortunately does not extend to racial issues. Blacks appear in *The Jungle* only as dissolute "scabs," used by the bosses for short periods and quickly discarded: "The ancestors of these black people had been savages in Africa, and since then they had been chattel slaves, or had been held down by a community ruled by the traditions of slavery. Now for the first time they were free—free to gratify every passion, free to wreck themselves. They were wanted to break a strike, and when it was broken they would be shipped away, and their present masters would never see them again." This is consistent with the theme of enslavement that runs through the whole book, but Sinclair makes no effort to see these hapless strikebreakers as human beings in their own right. They are simply an alien mass who make solidarity harder to achieve, which was just the way many labor unions saw both blacks and immigrants. The prewar Socialist party was good and prophetic on many modern social issues—labor issues, women's issues, environmental concerns, welfare ideas, health regulations, consumer protection, monopolistic business practices—but was divided and generally quiescent on racial issues. "Until the mass migration of Negroes into Northern industrial centers during the World War," says James Weinstein, "the Socialist Party paid little attention to the Negro."

The party declined sharply in numbers and influence after the World War I. As in many other countries, a separate and more militant Communist party was formed after the Russian Revolution, organized along Leninist lines. The old freewheeling utopianism and reformism of the prewar Socialists were replaced by a rigid adherence to whatever the current Soviet reading of Marxist dogma happened to be. But Sinclair, in his long career, remained generally faithful to the socialist spirit of the earlier period. His theoretical abilities were limited, but his energy and genteel combativeness were inexhaustible. *The Jungle* made him so famous that he became a political force in his own right. When he put the profits from the novel into founding a utopian colony in New Jersey, it became a subject for news and gossip. (It burned down after four and a half months.) When his troubled first marriage broke up it caused a delicious scandal, which he feared might damage the fortunes of socialism.

Many times he used his enormous facility as an observer and writer to take on powerful private interests and explosive issues: the Rockefellers and the coal industry in *King Coal* (1917), the Teapot Dome scandal and the oil industry in *Oil!* (1927), and the Sacco-Vanzetti case in *Boston* (1928), all journalistic novels based, like *The Jungle*, on Sinclair's own arduous firsthand research. Between 1918 and 1927 he wrote a series of long polemical pamphlets on subjects like "the profits of religion," the state of journalism, and the educational system. (These deserve comparison to the personal journalism of I. F. Stone, the cultural criticism of Paul Goodman, and the muckraking of Ralph Nader in the 1950s and 1960s.)

During the 1940s Sinclair applied the same glib talent to twentieth-century history in a series of eleven thinly fictionalized thrillers. Built around an agent named Lanny Budd, whose adventures are as fantastic and improbable as those of James Bond, this series made Sinclair one of America's most popular authors, but it doomed his critical reputation once and for all. Typically, Sinclair's main point of pride was his accuracy. In his very genial and buoyant autobiography, published in 1962, he boasted that no one had yet corrected him on a historical detail.

As a political figure Sinclair's most important moment, after the initial impact of *The Jungle*, came in California in 1934, when he left the Socialist party and was nearly elected governor on the Democratic ticket, with a crusade to "End Poverty in California" (EPIC). Though he was defeated in a bitter mud-slinging campaign, his platform helped push the national New Deal leftward. After World War II Sinclair gradually receded into obscurity, but for four decades he had been the epitome of the radical writer and activist. However old-fashioned he had begun to seem to younger writers between the wars, he remained a figue of extraordinary authority for all those who experimented in a more socially oriented, more committed literature.

By the time Sinclair died in 1968, at the age of ninety, with some ninety books behind him, the sharp dividing line between fact and fiction, which he had never been willing to observe, had begun to break down. The social and political ferment of the 1960s gave impetus to literary mutations in the form of the nonfiction novel, the novel as history, the documentary novel, the New Journalism (using fictional techniques), and finally the novels that introduced real historical personages, usually in an ironic vein. Rigid aesthetic demarcations, by which even Sinclair's best work was judged impure as fiction, gave way before a much greater willingness to mingle factual materials and fictional inventions. Earnest and sentimental as they could sometimes be, Sinclair's journalistic novels had foreshadowed this new turn of the wheel, but he was still remembered more as a muckraker than as a creative writer and Socialist pioneer. At the age of eighty-nine he returned to the White House, where he had been the guest of both Theodore and Franklin Roosevelt, to watch Lyndon Johnson sign the Wholesome Meat Act of 1967. A wheel had come full circle, but it was not necessarily the most important wheel.

TIMOTHY COOK

Upton Sinclair's The Jungle *and Orwell's* Animal Farm: *A Relationship Explored*

Although George Orwell tells us that the idea of *Animal Farm* came from his actual experience of seeing a small boy easily controlling a huge carthorse with a whip, various scholars have suggested literary sources or precedents for his fable. These include a number of Kipling's short stories, the fourth book of Swift's *Gulliver's Travels*, and, least plausibly, a section of John Gower's tedious Latin complaint *Vox Clamantis*, cited by Sean O'Casey, who makes his dislike of *Animal Farm* and his scorn for those who think it original very clear.

Orwell was of course far too well read to have claimed "originality," in the narrow sense of his having been the first person to make use of the human-animal relationship for political or social commentary. As an Eton scholar he would have known that the tradition goes back at least as far as Aristophanes' *Birds*. More importantly, we know from his own writings how much he admired Swift, in particular *Gulliver's Travels*, where he would have found the relationship between man and horse devastatingly reversed; indeed it is interesting that Orwell felt the Houyhnhnm nation had reached "the highest stage of totalitarian organization," the stage when conformity becomes so general that there is no need for a police force. In other words, this nation has achieved an equine version of the ideal Party that Orwell was to make O'Brien look forward to in *Nineteen Eighty-Four.*

From *Modern Fiction Studies* 30, no. 4 (Winter 1984). © 1984 by Purdue Research Foundation.

The boot he imagines stamping forever on the human face is foreshadowed by the unshod hoof that keeps the Yahoos in permanent subjection. In this context the Houyhnhnms' simplified language, although not deliberately created, can be seen as a parallel to Newspeak in making certain thoughts impossible.

The resemblances between *Animal Farm* and Houyhnhnm land are superficial. The latter may or may not be, in Orwell's words, "about as good as [sic] Utopia as Swift could construct," but it certainly can be seen as one, whereas *Animal Farm* of course presents a version of something that has happened in the real world. Indeed, underlying O'Casey's dismissal of Orwell's importance as a writer and his scorn of critics who compare Orwell with Swift is his outraged reaction to what was really "original" in *Animal Farm*, Orwell's effective development of his farm analogy into a detailed and devastating exposé of the betrayal of the October Revolution in Russia, a revolution that for O'Casey and other Party members was still a glorious, untarnished achievement.

Like all myths about ideal societies, the myth of the socialist utopia began to lose its attractiveness once an opportunity to establish it had arisen. Eleven years before Soviet Russia had come into being, however, it was possible to believe with much more fervor in the myth's validity as the solution to man's miseries. When Upton Sinclair's *The Jungle* was published in 1906, readers, depressed by his grimly vivid account of the sufferings of exploited Lithuanian immigrants in Chicago's stockyards, could still thrill to the revolutionary message of the socialist speakers and theorists in its closing pages. Orwell certainly knew *The Jungle*, and I would argue that *Animal Farm* owes more of a debt to Sinclair's best-known novel than it does to any preceding beast fable or animal story. In certain respects it can be seen as his answer to the hopeful message of the earlier book, though it is doubtful that he consistently intended it as such. Although he admired Upton Sinclair for his grasp of facts, especially in *The Jungle*, he criticized Sinclair's novels as little more than political tracts with nonexistent plots and unconvincing characters. At one point he even goes so far as to dismiss Sinclair, among other writers, as a "a dull windbag."

Windy, in the sense that its rhetoric is overblown and that it makes the same points over and over again, *The Jungle* certainly is, but most people would find the first part, the misadventures of Jurgis Rudkus and his family as they struggle to survive amid the Chicago slaughterhouses and packing factories, anything but dull. Of that first part Sinclair wrote in his *Autobiography*, "I wrote with tears and anguish, pouring into the pages all the pain that life had meant to me. Externally, the story had to do with a family of stockyard workers but internally it was the story of my own family." Such passionate self-identification of the struggling young writer with his central characters has helped to keep *The Jungle* constantly in print to the present day, making the story carry more conviction that we find in much of Sinclair's later documentary fiction. It certainly made a great impression on Orwell, for he says of the Lithuanian family's experiences that they are "truly moving." The book is of course no beast fable, though the man-beast comparison is implicit from the start in its title. Like *Animal Farm*, *The Jungle* is written to demolish a myth, but in this case it is the opposing, and older, one of America as the promised land, the capitalist Zion, the myth enshrined in the inscription of the Statue of Liberty. This myth had brought Jurgis from his native, semifeudal Lithuania, ironically czarist-Russian dominated, to a system in which he soon finds himself as helpless, as uncomprehending, as the hogs queuing to be turned into the products of the huge Durham pork factory.

In his powerful description of the mechanical pork-making process, Sinclair stresses the individuality and the human qualities of the hogs, right up to the moment when, despite his "protest, his screams," each is seized by a fate that "cut his throat and watched him gasp out his life." Jurgis Rudkus, the strong, naive peasant who is the central figure of Sinclair's novel, turns away from the scene of slaughter with the words "Dieve—but I'm glad I'm not a hog!" He has only just arrived in Chicago, and that very morning he has been given his first job in the factory. Soon he will be married to his sweetheart, Ona Lukoszaite, and they will live in an apparently new house bought on credit, but by that time he will have begun to realize how little he matters in his new country.

Later, destitute, bereft of wife and children, he finds himself at a political meeting listening to the message of a speaker calling for the socialist revolution. The speech he hears is lengthy and highly emotional, contrasting the lot of the workers being "ground up for profits in the world wide mill of economic might" with that of the few thousand bosses living in their "palaces" on "the products of the labor of brain and muscle" of the whole of society. It ends with a stirring appeal to the audience of working men, twice compared to beasts of burden, to look forward to the moment when the great giant of oppressed Labor will break free from his chains. This final vision brings the audience to its feet in wild enthusiasm. A few moments later, when someone starts singing the *Marseillaise* and the whole crowd excitedly joins in, Jurgis is stirred as never before in his life. He seeks to learn more about socialism from the orator and is referred to a Polish tailor under whose guidance he learns about the system for which he has been working:

> To Jurgis the packers had been equivalent to fate; Ostrinski showed him that they were the Beef Trust . . . Jurgis recollected how, when he had first come to Packingtown, he had stood and

watched the hog-killing and thought how cruel and savage it was, and come away congratulating himself that he was not a hog; now his new acquaintance showed him that a hog was just what he had been—one of the packers' hogs.

These passages could well have provided Orwell, consciously or subconsciously, first with the idea of choosing pigs as the animals to lead his revolution and then with the essential elements in the rhetoric of old Major's speech, through which at the start of *Animal Farm* the animals are inspired to rebel against their human masters. Indeed, Sinclair's hog with his individual character, protesting and screaming as he gasps out his life, is surely the prototype of the young porkers who (Major tells them) "will scream your lives out at the block within a year," just as the singing of the *Marseillaise* at the end of the socialist's speech seems to foreshadow the singing of the animal liberation hymn *Beasts of England* when Major finishes his. Jurgis, the exploited "packer's hog," is moved by the occasion to take charge of his own destiny, just as the Manor Farm animals are, under the pigs' leadership.

Although some might feel that the ideas in these sections of Sinclair's book were readily available in any number of political tracts, Orwell's familiarity with *The Jungle* makes it possible that he had these passages, with their man-hog comparisons and their references to workers as beasts of burden, at the back of his mind when working on *Animal Farm*, and that his fable is in part an ironic and disillusioned response to the earlier work's propagandist enthusiasm, showing how cruelly deceptive the hopes of a socialist heaven on earth can be; indeed *Animal Farm* may be, in this sense, actually a sequel to *The Jungle*.

This possibility is greatly strengthened when we look at an earlier part of the book, where Jurgis and his family struggle to survive in Packingtown, ignorant of the forces that are controlling their destinies. Jurgis is one of the two strongest members of the group; the other is his cousin, the broad-shouldered, good-natured Marija, who has "a broad Slavic face with prominent red cheeks. When she opens her mouth it is tragical, but you cannot help thinking of a horse." Sinclair uses this image again in describing how the forelady at Marija's first job is attracted by her "combination of a face full of boundless good nature and the muscles of a dray horse." Later, when she loses her first job at the canning factory, she is again seen as "a human horse."

Jurgis also is described in terms of his strength, his "mighty shoulders and giant hands," his "broad back" and his "rolling muscles." The two cousins are the mainstays of their family and, until in one way or another they fall foul of the system, are valued by their bosses as workers. Indeed work is Jurgis' answer to every crisis. At the start of the novel Jurgis and his child-wife Ona discover that their *veselija* or wedding party is going to cost much more than expected because of swindles over the drink and because of the various subterfuges used by other members of the Lithuanian community, corrupted by residence in America, to avoid paying their traditional share of the costs. He turns to his wife and reassures her,

> "Little one," he said in a low voice "do not worry—it will not matter to us. We will pay them all somehow. I will work harder." That was always what Jurgis said. Ona had grown used to it as a the solution of all difficulties—"I will work harder."

When Ona discovers that the house a smooth-talking agent has persuaded them to buy, beside being hardly worth the money they are spending on it, is going to cost them more in interest than they can afford, Jurgis' response is similar: "Jurgis took it stolidly. He had made up his mind to it by this time. It was part of fate; they would manage it somehow. He made his usual answer, 'I will work harder.'" When eventually he is sent to prison for assaulting the trucker's boss whose mistress Ona had become, he is regarded by Duane, the cynical safe-breaker who is his cell companion, as "a sort of working mule."

In the giant Jurgis and the dray horse-like Marija, as they battle on stoically and uncomprehendingly in an alien world in the early part of the book, we surely have human prototypes for Orwell's two carthorses Boxer and Clover, like them representatives of the true workers and victims of forces they do not understand. Indeed the resemblance to Jurgis as Orwell describes Boxer in the following passage surely goes beyond coincidence:

> Boxer with his tremendous muscles always pulled them through. He had been a hard worker even in Jones's time, but now he seemed more like three horses than one; there were days when the entire work of the farm seemed to rest upon his mighty shoulders. . . . His answer to every problem, every setback was "I will work harder!"—which he had adopted as his personal motto.

As with Sinclair's Jurgis, the motto is repeated several times in the book. It is on Boxer's lips as he works on the rebuilding of the windmill before his final collapse. However, whereas Jurgis becomes aware long before the end of *The Jungle* that all his work and sweat and agony has simply gone toward strengthening a system in which he is regarded as entirely expendable, Boxer only realizes the true nature of his situation too late, when he is trapped in the knacker's van on the way to a slaughterhouse that is real rather than metaphorical, betrayed by those very pigs with whom he has cooperated in bringing about an animal version of that revolution to which Sinclair's speaker, with his reiterated comparison of the workers to beasts of burden, had looked forward. Jurgis' creator, writing in 1906, could not know that when Marxism did have the opportunity to triumph it would not be in capitalist America but in relatively undeveloped Czarist Russia, and that the results of that triumph would be simply that one tyranny would be replaced by another. His message therefore ends in hope for the Jurgises of this world. Orwell, writing with hindsight, describes similar sufferings on his postrevolutionary farm, with far greater economy in words and with a much lighter tone, but can offer no hope because he had seen how irredeemably the power won had corrupted its holders. Indeed the despotism of the pigs of *Animal Farm*, as Bernard Crick has pointed out, foreshadows the ever harsher and much more somberly depicted tyranny of the Inner Party in *Nineteen Eighty-Four*.

It is perhaps worth mentioning one or two other ways in which the experiences of Boxer and the other animals under the pigs resemble those of Jurgis and his family in *The Jungle*. In *Animal Farm* we have, as a central symbol of their hopes for a life free of arduous labor in an animal commonwealth, the windmill planned by Snowball but worked on after his expulsion. In *The Jungle* we have that supreme symbol of the property-owning democracy of which Jurgis and his family consider themselves independent members: the "house of their own" that Jurgis and Ona are talked into buying. Both the windmill and the house become causes of endless heartbreaking work; both help to bring about the catastrophe in the life of the major character.

The reactions of Jurgis, on coming out of prison to find that the house is now irrevocably lost, closely parallel those of the animals when they find their windmill destroyed. The relevant passage in *The Jungle* ends as follows: "All that they had paid was gone—every cent of it. And their house was gone—they were back where they had started from, flung out into the cold to starve and freeze."

Against it, for comparison, let us put the thoughts of the animals as they contemplate the ruin of their hopes by Jones's dynamite:

> For a little while they halted in sorrowful silence at the place where the windmill had once stood. Yes it was gone; almost the last trace of their labour was gone! . . . It was as though the windmill had never been!

Although anyone studying these sections of the two books in their entirety will find a vast difference between Sinclair's windy rhetoric and the economy with which Orwell, writing with the relative detachment of the satirical fabulist, describes the scene, the emotional and structural correspondence between the separate situations remains striking.

Further parallels exist between the two books. Boxer's unsuccessful struggle to learn the alphabet is reminiscent of Jurgis' early struggle to read and speak English and indeed of his whole struggle toward political awareness. The accident that leads directly to the final destruction of Jurgis' hopes of happiness for himself and his family—making him recognize that he is now "second-hand, a damaged article so to speak—they had worn him out . . . and now they had thrown him away" and forcing him to work in the human scrapheap of the fertilizer plant—has its counterpart in the collapse of Boxer to which the pigs respond by selling him to the knacker's yard.

Both writers keep us constantly aware of the time of year. We move from one season to the next, each bringing its own problems but none more so than winter. If we compare the passage in Chapter Seven of *The Jungle*, beginning "Now the dreadful winter had come upon them," likening the workers to "cogs in the great packing machine," and describing the bitter winds and snowdrifts that they had to face, with Orwell's account of the "bitter winter" that followed the first collapse of the windmill, we will perceive an underlying similarity of technique despite the world, or at least ocean, of difference between Sinclair's Chicago and Orwell's rural England. If Orwell seems to lack indignation as he does metaphors of the emotive kind used by Sinclair, it is because his purpose is not to inform or to arouse, as Sinclair's is. He is working with facts that are already known but presenting them in a new guise. He knows that he does not need to stir up indignation by being indignant himself. He is confident that outrage will come after we have watched the animals endure so much while building the mill, which is used to grind corn for the financial benefit of the pigs and not to fulfill Snowball's vision of an easier life for every worker on the farm. The windmill, on one level a counterpart to the Rudkus house, can also be seen as Orwell's version of what Sinclair calls, in the passage just quoted, "the great packing machine" as a whole. Sinclair's two separate symbols are economically merged into one—as human jungle is transformed in Orwell's refining imagination to porcine dictatorship.

In her interesting comparison of Orwell with Sinclair, the only significant one, I believe, in any book published on Orwell to date (indeed Sinclair's name is not mentioned in Crick's recent biography, the Meyers' critical bibliography, or any work known to me that explores Orwell's relationship with the Left), Jenni Calder mentions *The Jungle* appreciatively although making just criticisms of its style, tone, and technique. However, the works she chooses for comparison with Sinclair's novels, of which she mentions several, are the novels and nonfictional works that Orwell wrote before *Animal Farm*. After discussing Orwell's views on Sinclair, she comes to the conclusion that "Orwell's sensitivity to the adulteration of literature by propaganda probably explains why he himself refrained from attempting to deliver a directly political message in his novels, except in the form of allegory and science fiction." In fact it is to what she calls Orwell's "allegory" that we should turn if we want to find clear evidence of the deep impression *The Jungle* made on him. It is also probable that the sense of hopelessness and squalor communicated by the first part of *The Jungle*, with its adulterated food, its cheap liquor, and its uncomprehending, helpless beast-of-burden like inhabitants, contributed something to Orwell's *Nineteen Eighty-Four* prole world with its shabby streets, poor food, and Victory gin. Orwell's striking ability to create vivid pictures through unpleasant factual detail, already evident in his earlier books and essays and regarded by a recent critic as a disagreeable feature of his work, may also owe much to his study of *The Jungle*.

Interestingly, Sinclair, after maintaining his socialist beliefs throughout the first four decades of the twentieth century, giving wholehearted support to the Russian Revolution, and being actively involved in such causes célèbres of the Left as the Sacco and Vanzetti affair and, at a distance, the Spanish Civil War, worried toward the end of his life perhaps even more than the dying Orwell about the threat to human happiness and liberty posed by left-wing totalitarianism. Indeed he even went as far, in 1953, as describing the activities of Senator Joseph McCarthy as less bad than communism. His disillusionment comes out in his late novel *The Return of Lanny Budd*, which, as Jon A. Yoder has rightly observed, shows that the Cold War destroyed him both as a liberal and as an effective propagandist.

As to Sinclair's reaction to Orwell's late writings, there is little evidence available to English readers out of reach of the Sinclair archives. However, it is surely significant that, five years before his death, when his massive anthology of literary extracts and documentary evidence about man's struggle for individual liberty, *The Cry for Justice*, was reissued in a new edition, one of the pieces added to it was the O'Brien speech from *Nineteen Eighty-Four*, that chilling vision of the boot on the human face referred to at the beginning of this article.

Returning, finally, to Orwell's own account of the genesis of *Animal Farm*, we must of course accept that the incident of the boy and the carthorse that he describes provided, either as a fresh experience or as a memory, the initial impulse that set him writing his fable. Nevertheless, the traces found in it of the impression made on his imagination by Sinclair's powerful radical novel seem clear enough to deserve acknowledgement.

R. N. MOOKERJEE

Muckraking and Fame: The Jungle

Upton Sinclair was one of the few lucky authors who found themselves famous overnight with a single book. *The Jungle* quickly made the unknown, struggling Sinclair a national celebrity and brought him not only a handsome financial reward of $30,000, but also hundreds of lecture invitations from all over the United States. Even the U.S. president, Theodore Roosevelt, invited him to the White House for discussions.

Ever since its first publication in 1906, *The Jungle* has remained an American classic, with 13 different editions and reprinting almost every year; outside the United States, the novel has been read by millions of readers, with translations in 34 languages. Even today, long after the events it described have become a part of history, *The Jungle* continues to have a hold on the imagination of an entirely new generation of readers. In a way, the book has a pointed relevance to our times. As Harvey Swados says:

> There is a close parallel between the payment in hunger, blood, and agony of the peoples of the under developed world and that extracted from the immigrant builders of the American empire. . . . *The Jungle* will help to sustain in the forefront of our consciousness, which is where it belongs.

From *Art for Social Justice: The Major Novels of Upton Sinclair.* © 1988 by R. N. Mookerjee.

There is indeed a timelessness about the novel and its characters. Sir Winston Churchill, in one of his rare pieces of literary criticism, very rightly said of the novel and its creator:

> This shrewd delineator of character . . . this painstaking and careful exponent of detail . . . the really excellent and valuable piece of work which this terrible book contains. . . . It pierces the thickest skull and the most leathery heart. It forces people who never think about the foundations of society to pause and wonder.

The novel's tremendous success upon its publication hardly gives one an idea of the travails it had to undergo to find a publisher. The origin and final publication of the book itself make interesting reading.

I

Newspapers and weekly magazines had firmly established themselves in the early years of the century. To boost circulation and open a window onto the actual state of social institutions and industrial establishments, S. S. McClure, the editor of *McClure's Magazine*, had stumbled upon the idea of providing in his magazine reports, of political misrule and business corruption, with documented evidence. In 1902, he launched his experiment with a series of articles by Ida M. Tarbell on the Standard Oil Company. He soon found his circulation rising. The cue was taken up by other magazines, and Ida Tarbell and Lincoln Stevens were commissioned for more such assignments. They did considerable research and on-the-spot enquiry for their reports. Impressed by *Manassas* (published in 1904) and its author's sympathy for the underdog, the socialist weekly, the *Appeal to Reason*, approached Sinclair for writing on the topic of wage slavery. Sinclair had some experience of such writing as he had already published two articles in *Collier's*. At Sinclair's request, Fred D. Warren, the editor of *Appeal*, agreed to advance $500 for the serial rights of what Sinclair had planned to be a novel based on life in the Chicago stockyards. As Sinclair himself recounted: "The recent strike had brought the subject to my thoughts, and my manifesto, 'You have lost the strike,' had put me in touch among the stockyard workers."

Sometime in autumn 1904, he set out for Chicago. He was to spend seven weeks there, collecting materials and making himself familiar with the scene and reality of the place, the locale of his novel.

Poorly dressed and with a dinner pail in his hand, he moved about everywhere in the Chicago stockyard, talking and exchanging notes with scores of workers. He also keenly and accurately observed everything that he saw and took extensive notes. The scene he witnessed was vividly impressed on his mind: By the end of the month he could say, "I had my data, and knew the story I meant to tell, but I had no characters." This may sound like a rather unusual way of beginning a novel since most novelists very often begin with certain characters in mind. However, in Sinclair's case, it should not be surprising that after the data has been collected and the story planned, he should be looking for characters, who, as will be seen later in the chapter, are not important for his purpose. He finally was able to get his characters when, toward the end of his stay, he witnessed a Lithuanian wedding in one of the saloons: "There were my characters—the bride, groom, the old mother and father, the boisterous cousin, the children, three musicians, everybody. I watched them one from another, and fitted them into my story, and began to write the scene in my mind."

On his return from Chicago, he built a broad cabin, eight feet by ten, set on a hillside north of Princeton, New Jersey, and started work on *The Jungle* on Christmas Day, 1904. This was the period during which Sinclair was passing through intense mental agony from financial worries and the responsibility of bringing up a child. Much of this suffering went into the novel, and to quote Sinclair himself:

> I wrote with tears and anguish, pouring into the pages all the pains which life had meant to me. Externally the story had to do with a family of stockyard workers, but internally it was the story of my own family. Did I wish to know how the poor suffered in winter time in Chicago? I had only to recall the previous winter in the cabin, when we had only cotton blankets, and had put rugs on top of us, and cowered shivering. . . . It was the same with hunger, with illness, with fear. "Ona" was "Corydon" [his wife Meta], speaking Lithuanian but otherwise unchanged. Our little boy was down with pneumonia that winter, and nearly died, and the grey of that went into the book.

Sinclair worked hard and incessantly on the story throughout the winter, spring, and summer of 1905, "sometimes blinded by his own tears." Although a major part of *The Jungle* was published in weekly installments (from February 1905 to November 1905) in the *Appeal to Reason*, which had a circulation of half a million, the novel had been completed before serialization, and hence one does not find in it the usual features of a serialized novel. *The Jungle* is shorter than Sinclair's other novels, there are no discrepancies, and a consistent pattern and technique is evident. In its issue of November 18, the *Appeal* published *"The Jungle:* A statement Concerning a Publication Plan," with an appeal by Sinclair for advance payment from his readers. Jack London also made an impassioned appeal for support in its publication by Sinclair himself since it had been refused by five publishers—including the Macmillan Co.—which had first agreed to publish it and even advanced $500 but later wanted certain portions to be deleted, which Sinclair refused.

Jack London's appeal was mainly directed toward the working class and was full of hope in the book's potential power to bring about change:

> The "uncle Tom's cabin" of wage slavery! . . . Comrade Sinclair's book, "The Jungle!" The beautiful theoretics of Bellamy's "Looking Backward" are all very good. They served a purpose, and served it well. . . . But I dare to say that "The Jungle," which has no beautiful theoretics, is even a greater book. It is alive and warm. It is brutal with life. It is written of sweat and blood, and groans and tears. It depicts not what man ought to be, but what man is compelled to be in this, our world, in the twentieth century. . . . It is written by an intellectual proletarian. . . . It will open countless ears that have been deaf to socialism. It will plough the soil for the seed of our propaganda. It will make thousands of converts to our cause.

The appeals had very encouraging response, 12,000 orders poured in and the book was put into type. At this point, Doubleday, Page and Co. showed an interest and offered to publish the book provided they could be satisfied as to its truth. Hence, from the beginning, the novel was taken to be an exposure of actual conditions rather than a piece of fiction unrelated to factual reality. After satisfying their concern for the authenticity of the book's main facts by sending their lawyer to Chicago, Doubleday published *The Jungle* in February 1906. It created a sensation almost immediately and shook the entire nation in a way few books had.

In a way, *The Jungle* could be taken as the fictional counterpart of the many journalistic nonfiction exposés so popular in those days. Jack London had talked of the book as the "seed of our (socialist) propaganda" that will "make thousands of converts to our cause." Sinclair, however, had no such motive at the time he went to Chicago to work on the book. Soon after the success of the novel, he clarified the purpose behind his writing:

> As a rule, the Muckrake Man began his career with no theories, as a simple observer of facts known to every person at all "in the

inside" of business and politics. But he followed the facts, and
the facts always led him to one conclusion; until he finally
discovered to his consternation that he was enlisted in a revolt
against capitalism.

Sinclair wanted to give vent to his sense of revulsion and horror generated
by the system. Fired by the Shelleyan spirit to wreck the old and prophesy
the advent of the Golden Future, he was looking for a form which would
enable him to move people powerfully. This Sinclair found in Zola, who had
enlarged the field of the novel with a vigor and audacity not known before.
Sinclair sought to combine what he had learnt from the two and tried, as he
himself said, to "put the content of Shelley into the form of Zola." It is also
very likely that he was familiar with the English working-class novel as it was
written towards the end of the nineteenth century, at least with Gissing, and
the impact of Zola's naturalism on these novels. He, therefore, placed his
findings in Chicago in a lifelike framework involving a poor, simple, just-
arrived immigrant group all agog with hope and confidence for a happy life
in America, where the profit motive had become the supreme objective.

During the closing decades of the nineteenth and the early years of the
twentieth centuries, immigration from European countries into America was
in full swing. According to one estimate, during this period "fifteen million
immigrants—an ever increasing proportion of them from southern and
eastern Europe—poured into the Promised Land, and great cities like New
York, Chicago, Pittsburgh, Cleveland, and Detroit doubled and redoubled
their size." Lured by the American dream of success, these poor immigrants
had come full of hope and aspiration for a happy life in their new country.
What was in store for them, however, was something completely different.
With changed conditions in the United States, for which Sinclair held the
capitalists responsible, all that these hapless people were offered was a nightmarish existence. Of all the immigrant groups, the Lithuanians, who were
simple, honest workers believing in "work and more work," were the worst
sufferers. The qualities that they held as their ideals and tried to attain,
however, were not those that now led to success and prosperity.

Sinclair was determined to expose the brutality and inhumanity that
the ordinary workers of America, who gave the nation all its wealth by the
sweat of their labor, suffered. He, therefore, chose this group from which to
draw his characters and story. Dedicating his novel "To the working men of
America," he performed a near miracle in his choice of the title, *The Jungle*,
which symbolized the absence of all civilized norms and the basic principles
of justice and fair play that constituted the bedrock upon which the
Founding Fathers had built the nation. The title, "A feat of imaginative

compression," as Walter Rideout put it, is also at once a severe indictment of the Darwinian philosophy of the survival of the fittest.

Sinclair felt that he must honestly and fearlessly present a naked picture of the conditions prevailing in the industrial world. He wanted to represent this world, in the novel, by a small segment of the meat-packing industry of Chicago, where the primitive laws of the jungle prevailed in the heart of industrialized America. According to Sinclair's analysis, in this jungle the fruits of the advance of science and technology resulting in vastly increased national resources were enjoyed only by the privileged, who heartlessly exploited the helpless masses of workers. In the packing town and its goings-on, Sinclair found the story he was looking for in all its details.

II

The Jungle opens in a Chicago saloon with the celebration following the marriage of Jurgis Rudkus, "with the mighty shoulders and the giant hands," to Ona Lukoszaite, "the blue-eyed and fair" 16-year-old girl whom Jurgis had met back in Lithuania. At that time he had been refused her hand because her father considered him too poor and his daughter rather young. But adversity soon struck her family. Her father died, leaving Ona, her step-mother, Elzbieta, and six children with no means of support.

At the suggestion of her uncle, Jonas, they decided to leave their native country for America, where they hoped to find work and happiness. Jurgis decided to follow Ona and came to "America and marry, and be a rich man in the bargain." Not only prosperity, but, in that country, he had heard "rich or poor, a man was free . . . a place of which lovers and young people dreamed."

After being cheated at two places, this group of 12 immigrants which also included Marija, Ona's stepmother's cousin, finally reach Chicago and find lodging at Mr. Jukniene's "unthinkably filthy" home. But the expectant immigrants do not mind. Jurgis finds a job, as the others gradually do. Soon Jurgis takes a house on installment, vowing to work still harder. However, the contact is rigged—a single missed payment could deprive Jurgis of his home. The happiness of the immigrant is short lived: a severe winter against which these poor people had no protection claims the lives of Jurgis's father and Ona's stepbrother; Marija loses her job; Jurgis's income, despite longer hours of work, is considerably reduced; Ona is left with "womb-trouble" after the birth of her son, Antanas. Conditions for them became worse when the second winter arrives. Ona becomes too sick to go to work, while Jurgis himself is badly hurt at the "Killing-bed." He is laid off for two weeks, and just at this time Uncle Jones, too, leaves them. Even after recovering, Jurgis is too weak to stand on his legs and loses his job. It is only after two months that he finds employment in a filthy fertilizer plant. Ona and Jurgis start drifting apart under the blow of one tragedy after another, and the worst happens when Ona, in order to save her job, agrees to sleep with her boss. Jurgis, mad with rage when he comes to know of his wife's seduction, assaults Ona's seducer. He is arrested and sent to jail for a month. On his release he finds his home sold to someone else and finally locates Ona in the cheapest garret of a boardinghouse, suffering intense agony in childbirth, and dying. Her death at the age of 18 shattered Jurgis's dreams of happiness and changed the course of the rest of his life: "An icy horror of loneliness seized him; he saw himself standing apart and watching all the world fade away from him—a world of shadows, of fickle dreams." After much effort, Jurgis manages to find a job first at the Harvester plant and then in a steel mill, a welcome change of work from the killing beds. But this proves short lived as he hurts his fingers and is laid off for a week. He takes to begging and drinking, and the ruin for him is complete when his son, Antanas, is drowned in the mud of Chicago's streets. Speechless and almost mad for a time, he becomes a cynic. He moves out of Chicago, and for the summer goes into the countryside. The contrast that the peace and quiet of the streams and simple farmhouses provide restores Jurgis to a normal state: his "health came back to him, all his youthful vigor, his joy and power that he had mourned and forgotten." As winter approaches and he can no longer continue his life as a tramp, he returns to Chicago. He gets employment in the digging of freight tunnels. He had already deserted Ona's relatives and was leading the life of a hobo. He undergoes a short jail sentence again when he assaults a bartender. But this time he meets a professional thief in prison, through whom he comes into contact with the criminal underworld and politically powerful bosses. He soon learns the way of success and rises rapidly to become a "foreman" in the same firm that had dismissed him. For some time he changes, taking on the degrading values he once detested so much. But pangs of conscience haunt him, and when accidentally he comes across the man who had ruined Ona's life, he attacks him brutally. But things have changed this time. Now Jurgis is not friendless, he has political support and does not have to go to jail. However, when his bosses realize that he is not of much use to them, he is dropped. Jurgis finds himself back to the life of a tramp in the soulless big city: begging, stealing, drinking, seeking a new shelter every night. At this stage he meets Marija, whose fate, no different from his, has turned her into a prostitute. She is not ashamed of it because, as she says, "we can't help it." Jurgis is told that Stanislovas, Ona's stepbrother, is dead, and the remaining members of the family live on Marija's earnings.

Marija persuades Jurgis to accept her help and almost forces him to go to Ona's people. Jurgis, however, is reluctant to face them after what he had done. In this state of indecision, he finds himself walking down a hall where a political speech is being delivered. He enters the hall but, least interested in what is going on, he goes off to sleep when "suddenly came a voice in his ear, a woman's voice, gentle and sweet. 'If you would try to listen, comrade, perhaps you would be interested.'" Jurgis is overwhelmed by the attention he receives and listens intensely to the long speech and at the end shouts along with others because "the stress of his feeling was more than he could bear" and also because he had heard "a voice with strange intonations that rang through the chambers of the soul like the clanging of a bell." Jurgis is now aware of socialism and is guided further in socialist thought by comrade Ostrinski. On hearing Jurgis's story, comrade Ostrinski exclaims: "We will make a fighter out of you!"

With his newfound passion for socialism, Jurgis has no hesitation in going to Elzbieta and the family. In a week's time he is able to get employment as a porter in the small hotel of Tonny Hinds, "the best boss in Chicago. . . . State organizer of [socialist] party." With all his heart and soul, Jurgis joins other socialist workers to spread the movement. His unhappiness on account of the loss of his family does not matter any longer for "he could solace himself with a plunge into the socialist movement." Then follows a long debate about the meaning of socialism, the relationship of religion and capitalism, and of socialism and Christianty. Through comrade Lucas, a religious person "who knew only the Bible, but it was the Bible interpreted by real experience," Sinclair gives expression to his own view of socialism, a kind of Christian socialism:

> "This Jesus of Nazareth!" he cried, "This class-conscious working-man! This union carpenter! This agitator, law-breaker, fire-brand, anarchist! He, the sovereign lord and master of a world which grinds the bodies and souls [of] human beings into dollars—if [he] could come into the world this day and see the things that men have made in his name, would it not blast his soul with horror? Would he not go mad at the sight of it, he the Prince of Mercy and Love!"

The novel ends with a socialist election speech that holds out a promise of better days: "And we shall organize them, we shall drill them, we shall marshal them for victory! We shall back down the opposition, and we shall sweep it before us—and Chicago will be ours! *Chicago will be ours!* CHICAGO WILL BE OURS!"

From the rather detailed foregoing account, it is clear that, so far as the story of *The Jungle* is concerned, it is essentially a straight narrative centered around the hope, vicissitudes, and finally hope again of a single character, Jurgis Rudkus. All 31 chapters of the novel are in someway or another connected with him or with events and places with which he is involved. In a sense, this would imply that Sinclair was adopting, as Bloodworth suggests, "the classic naturalistic pattern of inexorable movement towards chaos and doom." However, Sinclair, opposed as he was to the basic mechanistic and deterministic philosophy of naturalism that accepted such suffering as inherent in the laws of nature, used the pattern to expound his socialist philosophy. He sought to show that it was the system under which the working class became a pawn in the hands of the unscrupulous, greedy rich that was responsible for all the suffering and misery. Before one examines the structure and other fictional devices Sinclair employed, one must take into consideration his underlying purpose in writing the novel, and the problems such writing inevitably entail.

Broadly speaking, Sinclair's main purpose in writing *The Jungle* was to focus attention on the inhuman and sordid conditions in which the American wage earner lived and worked. Had he been content with this alone, he would not have, like Zola in *L'Assommoir* (1877), faced any artistic problem in the fusion of his materials into an organic unity. However, Sinclair added two more objectives: to fix the responsibility for such a horrifying state on the capitalist system, and to show that the only hope of bringing about a change was the advent of socialism. As an artist he faced his greatest problem in achieving his second objective since the demands of artistic structure and impartiality and the call of socialism are difficult to reconcile. But such problems of harmonization are inherent in these sorts of ideologically oriented novels, and one would be well advised to accept this and not expect something that the very nature and purpose of such writing seldom allows. Zola's *L'Assommoir*, which is regarded as the "archetypal late nineteenth-century slum novel," offers a fine example of this problem. Keating, in his study, suggests that the "various artistic problems . . . the English working class novelists were struggling with, are triumphantly solved [in Zola]." This is obviously a reference to Zola's artistic success in "standing aside from the central action of the book (*L'Assommoir*) and allowing everything to be defined in terms of '*les moeurs du people*.'" But while succeeding in this, Zola fails on the ideological side by refusing to offer political or social or even humanitarian comment. The same is true of Zola's other novel, *Germinal*, which, as Hemmings points out, Marxist critics refuse to accept as "constituting evidence that Zola contemplated an ultimate dictatorship of the proletarist." In his treatment of the working class in his novels, Zola, in deference to artistic demands, is neither a revolutionary nor a reactionary. By remaining carefully and intentionally neutral, Zola left unexamined the full implications and significance of the social issues that he raised while he succeeded immensely in making their existence and gravity blindingly clear. Sinclair wanted to do both, and for him the ideological part was the more important.

In being so motivated, Sinclair followed George Bernard Shaw, whose plays and other writings he had read and admired and who had openly declared that his intention was to convert people to his ideas through his plays. Though Sinclair often talked of putting the spirit of "Shelley into the form of Zola," it would be more appropriate to say that he was trying to put the Shavian spirit into a naturalistic form. Like Shaw, Sinclair, too, openly acknowledged that the primary purpose of his art was to move the reader to action. He was not interested in producing an aesthetically satisfying work. The dominance of the elements of argumentation and narration in Sinclair's work, therefore, follows from his purpose as a creative writer.

Another problem that such polemical writing entails is that of the point of view of the author. This, in Sinclair's case was predetermined. Though he himself did not belong to the working class, he wrote essentially from their point of view, and most often his voice and that of his protagonist, Jurgis, are identical. In fact, since Jurgis for quite some time in the novel has no voice of his own (he has yet to learn English), the author himself supplies his voice.

In structuring his novel, Sinclair adapted the basic pattern of Zola. The first 22 chapters wherein the various stages of Jurgis's career from hope to despair and nightmare are traced through a series of powerful descriptive passages are reminiscent of the best naturalistic writing. Sinclair adhered to direct observation as closely as possible and avoided details that could not be supported by evidence. His superb choice of characters drawn from the poorest and weakest of the working classes (the new immigrants from eastern Europe who did not even know the English language) and placed in the stifling environment of the packing town enabled Sinclair to succeed in creating a feeling of utter revulsion with existing conditions.

In the opening scenes of *The Jungle*, Sinclair uses the device of flashback. After Sinclair describes the marriage feast, chapters II, III, and VI go back in time and narrate the history of the Lithuanian group, as well as describe in detail the physical setting of the packing establishments, from the cattle pens to finished meat packages. Chapter VII resumes the link with chapter I, and the next four chapters are devoted to an account of the trials and tribulations of Jurgis and the other members of his family. No significant action in the unfolding of the story takes place till chapter XVII, when Jurgis comes to know of Ona's seduction. His assault on Ona's seducer lands him in jail. From this point to chapter XXIV, when Jurgis meets Master Freddie, it is, except for the brief spell in the countryside, a repetition of the same account of poverty, starvation, and suffering. A slightly varying note is struck in chapters XXVI to XXVIII, when Marija is brought back and the issue of prostitution and poverty raised. Chapter XXVIII also begins what may be called the last segment, dealing with the message of socialism as the only remedy for the jungle created by the capitalist system.

From this brief account of the plan on which Sinclair proceeds, "the utter destruction of the whole family in circumstances of misery and horrid degradation," as Sir Winston Churchill in one of his rare articles on literary criticism put it, it would be obvious why he followed a straight chronological narrative in the manner of the historical novel for the major part of *The Jungle*. This technique was also one of Sinclair's strongest points as an artist. It allowed him scope to develop and perfect the documentary mode of novel writing that he was to adopt for all his major novels. Much in the manner of journalistic reporting of actual conditions with appropriate modifications for its fictionalization, "here in *The Jungle*," as Alfred Kazin remarked, "was the great news story of a decade written out in letters of fire. Unwittingly or not, Sinclair had proved himself one of the great reporters of the Progressive Era, and the world now began to look up to him as such."

Since Sinclair's major concern was to move his readers with the horrifying truth of the actual conditions of the worker's life and work, he made extensive use of the device of packing his narrative with the minutest details and of piling up massive word pictures, so popular with naturalists like Dreiser and Norris. Sinclair's account goes on and on until the reader has the impression of being completely enveloped by the atmosphere of this horror-filled world. Everything is shown as seen and felt by Jurgis or by one of the other similarly afflicted characters. Sinclair begins using this device early in the novel. This is how the Chicago stockyards are described:

> The roadway was commonly several feet lower than the level of the houses, which were sometimes joined by high boardwalks; there were no pavements—there were mountains and valleys and rivers, gullies and ditches, and great hollows full of stinking green water. In these pools the children played, and rolled about in the mud of the streets; here and there one noticed them digging in it, after trophies which they had stumbled on. One wondered about this, as also about the swarms of flies which hung about the scene, literally blackening the air, and the strange, fetid odor, of all the dead things of the universe.

The fertilizer plant where Jurgis worked after his illness is presented thus:

The Fertilizer works of Durham's lay away from the rest of the plant. Few visitors ever saw them, and the few who did would come out looking like Dante, of whom the peasants declared that he had been into hell. To this part of the yards came all the "tankage," and the waste products of all sorts; here they dried out the bones—and in suffocating cellars where the daylight never came, you might see men and women and children bending over whirling machines and sawing bits of bone into all sorts of shapes, breathing their lungs full of the fine dust, and doomed to die, every one of them, within a certain definite time. Here they made the blood into albumen, and made other foul-smelling things into things still more foul-smelling. In the corridors and caverns where it was done, you might lose yourself as in the great caves of Kentucky.

There are other passages that caused the great public furor about the quality of meat—an issue far removed from Sinclair's intention:

There were the wool pluckers, whose hands went to pieces even sooner than the hands of the pickle men. . . . There were those who made the tins for the canned meat, and their hands too, were a maze of cuts, and each cut represented a chance for blood poisoning . . . as for the other men, who worked in tank rooms full of steam, and in some of which there were open vats near the level of the floor, their peculiar trouble was that they fell into the vats; and when they were fished out, there was never enough of them left to be worth exhibiting—sometimes they would be overlooked for days, till all but the bones of them had gone out to the world as Durham's Pure Leaf Lard!

Even supplies to the U.S. army were not spared, and Sinclair unraveled the mystery of many deaths:

There were cattle which had been fed on "Whisky malt," the refuse of the breweries, and had become what the men called "steerly"—which means covered with boils. . . . It was stuff such as this that made the "embalmed beef" that had killed several times as many United States soldiers as all the bullets of the Spaniards; only the army beef, besides, was not fresh canned, it was old stuff that had been lying for years in the cellars.

These scenes are powerful, and the novel, as the *Literary History of the United States* says, "develops a cumulative power; its lurid melodramatic climaxes come alive with the grotesque conviction of nightmare. Little in Zola or Dostoyevsky surpasses the nightmarish strength of the scenes. . . ."

Such graphic descriptions had a tremendous effect and attracted readers and critics on both sides of the Atlantic. Sir Winston Churchill, then a young member of the British Parliament, was so moved that he wrote a long two-part review of the novel to "make it better known" and said:

> The worst has been told and only the worst; it has been told in the most effective way, and the reader is confronted—nay over-whelmed. . . . Let me say at once that people have no right to hold their noses and shut their eyes. If these things are true, all honour to him who has the power and skill to fasten world-wide attention upon them. If they be only half-true, a great public service has been rendered.

By a very clever arrangement and juxtaposition of such scenes with the narrative of Jurgis's career, Sinclair makes these an important and integral element in his argument against a system that permits such abuses. As Winston Churchill rightly commented,

> nothing can exceed the skill and determination with which the author has marshalled his arguments. . . . All conditions of life—social, moral, political, economic, commercial, climatic, bacterio-logical are assembled, drilled into order, arranged under the proper standards and led by converging roads to the assault.

For the greater part of the novel, every point in the story is enriched by such vivid and realistic details; one is immersed in the filth and stench and cruelty of the stockyards. Yet one does not fail to notice beneath it all, however faint, sublime human aspirations that burn in humble hearts. It is this burning desire aided and encouraged by faith in the ultimate victory of social justice that gives new life to Jurgis and accounts for the optimistic ending of the novel.

Until chapter IX, when Jurgis becomes "desirous of learning English," none of the characters seem to know the language in which the novel is written. Therefore, for over a full quarter of the novel's length (nearly 150 pages), the author himself becomes the voice of the chief as well as the other characters. One reads in the novel a straight third-person narration, with about a dozen or so lines in broken English to lend an air of authenticity. This would appear to be rather unusual for a practitioner of the craft of fiction in the twentieth century. But not so for Sinclair, who found such reportorial writing more congenial. In fact this constitutes one of the significant aspects of

Sinclair's fictional techniques: His "voice" as a narrator. In writing so, he was using a major device of the nineteenth-century novel. In most of his novels, Sinclair tells his story in the third person and permits himself complete freedom both in what he knows and how he goes about informing us of what he knows. As a third-person omniscient narrator, he informs the reader directly about the characters and their situations and freely comments on social, economic, and other matters. Such authorial comments form substantial parts of most of the chapters in *The Jungle*. Like the nineteenth-century English novelists whom he had read and admired, Sinclair readily accepted the dominant role of an authorial presence in the art of the story-telling. In fact, he needed such a device so as to be able to have the freedom to argue his case against the ills of the social system of which the characters he portrayed were the helpless victims.

Sinclair's two most distinctive authorial voices in the novel are those of a faithful chronicler of events and background and a sympathetic commentator on his character's actions, angry at the injustices of an economic and political system that allowed unfettered exploitation of the working class. This practice is again in keeping with the nineteenth-century convention of the novelist as an epic narrator who not only represents but also discusses and gives his opinion on the underlying truths of society and human nature. As Sinclair comments early in the novel, all the cherished values of the Founding Fathers of the New World had been distorted. Jurgis had though that if he worked hard, with honesty, he would succeed. But he is very much mistaken,

> for nobody rose in Packing town by doing good work. You could lay that down for a rule—if you met a man who was rising in Packing town, you met a knave . . . the man who minded his own business and did his work—why, they would "speed him up" till they had worn him out, and then they would throw him into the gutter.

Toward the latter part of the novel, the insignificance and helplessness of the poor worker is made more explicit in a "world in which nothing counted but brutal might, an order devised by those who possessed it for the subjugation of those who did not."

Sinclair's characterization in *The Jungle* is governed by this view of the working-class world. Almost all his important characters are drawn from this class, and this choice, coupled with his basic conception, dictated the type of characters he could create. Powerful characters—characters who would overcome the mighty obstacles and emerge victorious—are ruled out; in fact, creating such characters would have defeated his purpose. But surely he had to portray men and women of flesh and blood who would put up a fight and act as human beings before the readers could be convinced of the unjustness of the system. And in doing this, Sinclair, despite charges of failure to have realized his characters as "living persons," has been quite successful. Jurgis Rudkus, around whose character and progress the entire novel revolves, certainly turns out to be a convincing character, except in the last four chapters, in which the change in him seems too sudden to be convincing. But Jurgis from his first appearance (chapter I) to his renewed determination to fight (ch. XXVIII) shows growth and change. His huge figure and physical strength are emphasized time and again as symbolic of the mighty worker. His actions are in keeping with his simplicity. He is the typical worker, who, despite heavy odds against him, fights back again and again. For a time Jurgis struggles with almost superhuman strength. He meets every difficulty by valiant answer, and we even think that he would eventually succeed. But events like the spraining of his ankle, the sudden closure of the factories, rendering him jobless; and the seduction of his wife finally break him; and for a time he gives up. What happens to Jurgis could happen to any worker under the system. For Sinclair, this was the most important truth, and this he tried to convey through his characterization of Jurgis.

Jurgis is not the only character in the novel who attracts attention. There are two other characters—both women—who are drawn with sympathy and insight and, by the time the novel ends, become realized characters. One is Marija, and the other Elzbieta, both of whom heroically stand up unshaken against poverty, death, desertion, and an unjust society. Marija, who takes to prostitution to support the family and educate the children, shows considerable growth, and our respect for her is enhanced. Elzbieta is the picture of the all-suffering, all-sacrificing, all-forgiving mother who, undaunted by the heavy odds against her, fights back. With each calamity, she seems to grow stronger and is the very incarnation of an infinite capacity to bear and suffer. It is surprising that studies of *The Jungle* have failed to take notice of these brave women and merely repeated the charge that Sinclair was unable to create convincing characters. Within the limited scope that characterization had in his novels, in view of his declared objectives, these characters are sufficiently developed to merit notice. In this respect, Sinclair is like the English problem playwrights who, in order to focus attention on social problems, could hardly afford to create powerful characters. Quite a few characters of Sinclair are like the characters of John Galsworthy, who belong to humble stations and are unable to overcome their social and economic handicaps.

Beyond a certain point, mainly in terms of narrative technique, Sinclair does not have much in common with Emile Zola. "His real affinity," as had been very rightly pointed out by Professor Rideout is with "the mid-victorian English reform novelists." Parts of *The Jungle* invariably remind the reader of Dickens, with whose work Sinclair was quite familiar. The appalling and shocking conditions of the industrial workers and the detailed descriptions of the Chicago industrial world echo similar scenes in *Hard Times*. The two writers also show resemblances in "presentation of character, in the tendency of both to intrude themselves with bubbling delight or horrified indignation into the scene described," and, most of all, in their intensely humanitarian approach. Despite his vigorous advocacy of socialism, Sinclair never gave up the Christian ideals imbibed in his early years. While Dickens did not bother to go deep into the problems created by industrialization and their possible solutions, and urged the practice of Christian ideals, Sinclair grappled with these issues and advocated a wholesale transformation of society through socialism. It is important to remember that even in *The Jungle*, the socialist remedy suggested in the last chapters is to be brought about by peaceful, democratic means. Violence and bloodshed were not the tools for Sinclair. The essential spirit behind him, as in Dickens, was one of intense humanitarianism and brotherly love.

In his use of language and imagery, Sinclair never allowed himself to forget that he was primarily writing for the literate or even semiliterate men and women of the working classes. This intention ruled out the use of any complex symbolism or experimentation in technique and, most of all, verbal economy. He had to gear his prose style to a level at which his common reader would have no difficulty in understanding, and the author could easily establish communication. This partly explains the lack of any particular brilliance in his language. However, throughout *The Jungle* one comes across smooth, flowing prose written with ease and felicity and, in its very simplicity, tremendously effective in moving his readers. On occasions, it even attains the somber dignity and sublimity equal to the human suffering and tragedy it sought to express. The realization by the Jurgis family of how they have been cheated out of everything is expressed thus:

> Then again there was not a sound. It was sickening, like a nightmare, in which suddenly something gives way beneath you, and you feel yourself sinking, sinking down into bottomless abysses. As if in a flash of lightening they saw themselves—victims of a relentless fate, cornered, trapped, in the grip of destruction. All the fair structures of their hopes came crashing about their ears—And all the time the old woman was talking. They wished that she would be still; her voice sounded like the croaking of some dismal raven. Jurgis sat with his hands clenched and beads of perspiration on his forehead, and there was a great lump in

Ona's throat, choking her. Then suddenly Teta Elzbieta broke
the silence with a wail, and Marija began to wring her hands
and sob.

Throughout the narrative, Sinclair makes effective use of simple similes and
appropriate adjectives to give variety to his otherwise journalistic, descriptive
style. Phrases like "mute agony," "hunted rabbit," "mountain forest lashed
out by a tempest," and "soul baked hard in the fire of adversity" prove
powerful in their contexts.

One, however, misses in Sinclair the rough and often ungenteel
diction one would expect from a working-class group. There are hardly any
swearwords or abuses, and one does not have the feel of low-class speech;
in fact, one is surprised by the prim propriety of speech displayed by his
working-class characters. One reason for this is perhaps that working-class
speech and dialogues in his novels are severely restricted because most of
the time the narrator-author himself does this job. Another reason is that
despite his championship of their case, Sinclair had never lived among the
working classes for any length of time to give him command over the
language they used. To this extent, Sinclair's depiction of working-class life
is deficient and unauthentic.

The ending of *The Jungle* has been the subject of discussion and
comment ever since its first publication. It is often cited as the chief fault of
the novel, and hardly any critic or reader seems to find it satisfactory.
Boynton held that "at the end of the story, the logic of events is suspended."
George J. Becker felt that "unfortunately for the novel, the author turns the
last third of it into a tract advocating socialism, with the final fifty pages
ceasing to be a story at all and becoming an harangue." According to Jon
Yoder, the last part is "tacked onto a plot that stops moving when Jurgis sits
down to listen." Bloodworth, in his recent study, also feels that in the last
chapters Sinclair destroyed the book's unity by shifting the "focus of his
novel from Jurgis to the Socialist movement itself."

There is no doubt that, from an artistic point of view, the last four
chapters remain unabsorbed in the overall structure of the novel and spoil an
otherwise powerful narrative of the colossal tragedy and destruction of
human values portrayed through the story of Jurgis in the first 27 chapters
(except for the digressions concerning Marija, chiefly in chapter XXVII).
This part certainly appears forced, and it is surprising that, instead of
working over these chapters again and achieving a proper harmony with the
rest of the novel, Sinclair should have rushed it into publication. More so
when he himself was dissatisfied as his letter to Wilshire clearly suggests.
Sinclair attributes this failure to his money problems: "Suffice it to say that

never have I been able to write a single thing as I would have liked to write it, because of money. . . . My whole life has been ruined in this way. My work has got poorer and poorer."

It is difficult to see the correlation unless he meant that because he needed money urgently, he rushed into publication and did not wait to rewrite and weave the socialist message into the texture of the novel. What really seems to have happened is that Sinclair had not originally planned to end the novel in this way. However, at the time he was completing it in 1905, he was also busy starting the Inter-Collegiate Socialist Society. He was so carried away with his enthusiasm for his newfound ideology that he could not resist putting in a plea for socialism and, hence, imposed these chapters even at the cost of impairing the unity of the structure of the book.

Even chapter XXVIII begins well and is able to sustain the reader's interest in the story. Unfortunately, somewhere in the middle of the chapter, Jurgis listens to the socialist oration and then, alas! Everything seems to be forgotten except the history and philosophy of socialism and how the move-ment could be carried on in America. For Sinclair himself, of course, the purpose of making his working-class readers conscious of their rights was far more important than aesthetic considerations. Nevertheless, since it was through an art form that Sinclair tried to achieve his purpose, he might as well have shown greater respect for the demands of "art," as did his friends like George Bernard Shaw and H. G. Wells. Socialism had already been intro-duced in the novel fairly early when the workers were becoming gradually aware of their exploitation (chapter V). Workers Unions and their meetings are described a little later, (chapter VIII) followed by numerous other refer-ences. With a little imagination he could still have conveyed his message without destroying the effect of a gripping story of human suffering. As Frank Harris wrote to Sinclair about the ending of the novel: "I think three quarters of *The Jungle* unsurpassable, extraordinary, magnificent, anything you like; any adjective is justified. But the end it seems to me should have flamed in some terrible revolt, and then the book would have been an epic." *The Jungle* was not destined to be an epic; at best it remains a flawed epic. "One must, however, concede in fairness to Sinclair that this failure to fuse fictional with political statement would appear to be pervasive in 'ideological' fiction of all stripes."

III

Quite apart from considerations of artistic and literary merit, *The Jungle* was an overwhelmingly popular and financial success. It remains to this day, and seems destined to remain for a long time to come, an important document of American life—however unpleasant and unpalatable. In addition, *The Jungle* demonstrated, as very few literary works had done before, to focus attention on issues of paramount interest to society.

The immediate cause that attracted nationwide attention to *The Jungle* and created all the hue and cry was the disclosures it made about the quality and mode of packing of meat supplied to millions of Americans by the giant establishments of Chicago. The consumer was horrified to know that what was sold as "pure beef" was in fact diseased meat unfit for human consumption. Obviously, *The Jungle* was not taken as a purely imaginative piece of work, but as an authentic account of actual conditions prevailing at the time. Hence, the American press and people, long before the advent of the journalistic novel of recent years—what Norman Mailer termed as "History as a Novel and Novel as History"—had, in fact, taken Sinclair's novel as a piece of investigative reporting. Not only this, it also proceeded to take follow-up action despite the meat packers' denials, which the public did not accept. So strong was the shock and protest that President Theodore Roosevelt had to take note of these revelations. He ordered the labor commissioner, Charles P. Neill, and the assistant secretary of the treasury, James B. Raynolds, to go to Chicago and investigate. Their report substantially endorsed Sinclair's accounts in *The Jungle*. The president acted immediately and signed the Federal Food and Drugs Act (popularly known as the "Pure Food Law"), which became effective on June 30, 1906. To this extent Sinclair's "muckraking" yielded positive results, and, like Galsworthy's *Justice*, which changed solitary imprisonment rules in England, *The Jungle* brought about an important piece of legislation. However, this was an incidental side effect and was never Sinclair's purpose. Despite the fame and money the book brought him, he felt a sense of failure. In an interview soon after the book's success in 1906, he expressed his feelings thus:

> I failed in my purpose, when you know of all the uproar that *The Jungle* has been creating. But then that uproar is all accidental and was due to an entirely different cause. I wished to frighten the country by a picture of what its industrial masters were doing to their victims; entirely by chance I had stumbled on another discovery—what they were doing to the meat supply of the civilized world. In other words, I aimed at the Public's heart, and by accident I hit it in the stomach.

Even the Act created in 1906 was soon diluted, and the business interests again had an upper hand. As regards Sinclair's primary objective of bringing about improvement in workers' living conditions, practically nothing was done to alleviate their lot.

But as a piece of imaginative writing, *The Jungle* was tremendously successful in one sense: It made thousands of workers and wage earners in American conscious of their conditions and gave them an awareness and hope of a better deal. Addressing its readers, the worker's organ of the times, *Young Worker*, had said of *The Jungle:* "it is more than just a story. It is an epic . . . [of our] struggle in America. If you haven't read it yet, don't eat your lunch tomorrow and buy this book." The fact that, despite neglect by literary critics, the novel has been read and an edition published almost every year for about three-quarters of a century now, testifies to the abiding interest in *The Jungle* as a moving, heartrending, and terrifying picture of what human beings, in a given setup, have done to other human beings.

EMORY ELLIOTT

Afterword to The Jungle

In spite of the phenomenal success of *The Jungle*, Upton Sinclair lamented what he considered to be its failure when he made his often-quoted assessment: "I aimed at the public's heart and by accident I hit it in the stomach." As is often the case with jokes, this seemingly flip remark contains more truths than are immediately apparent: it speaks directly to the purpose, techniques, and results of the novel. There is no question that Sinclair hit the feelings of large numbers of readers in 1906 when his book appeared and that his work has continued to generate powerful reactions throughout nearly a century. Still, strong disagreements among historians and critics persist over the nature of Sinclair's literary weapon, his intended target, and his aim.

In 1894, twelve years before he would become internationally famous at age twenty-seven as the author of *The Jungle*, Sinclair began his publishing career by writing jokes and short stories for New York City newspapers. Perhaps humor enabled him to deal with the painful family situation he endured. On his father's side, he descended from an aristocratic Virginia family in decline. His great grandfather had fought in the Revolution and had been one of the founders of the U.S. Naval Academy, but his own father was of the displaced generation of Southerners who lost both wealth and pride after the Civil War. As Sinclair's father succumbed to alcoholism, his mother, a stern Methodist, imparted her love of books and her hatred of all dependencies and indulgences to her son. After the family moved to New York in 1886, Sinclair earned money by writing while he attended school to help fight the family's poverty and to better his future chances.

After graduating from the City College of New York, Sinclair attended Columbia University, with the intention of becoming a lawyer, where he published hundreds of stories for young people. Through his reading, he developed a strong attachment to the Romantic literature of Shelley, Emerson, and others, and in 1896 he decided to embark upon a literary career. Both as a writer and as a person he was extremely divided: temperamentally, he had a Romantic longing for the noble family past and for the happy childhood he never had, while intellectually, he was beginning to question the values, traditions, and historical circumstances that hindered his own family and countless other Americans.

In the literary world of the mid-1890s, realism and naturalism were placing a new stress upon the role of the artist as recorder of the facts of daily life and as a potential leader of social reforms. Stephen Crane, Mark Twain, Frank Norris, Kate Chopin and others consciously used their pens to challenge nineteenth century attitudes and social conventions. In 1900, when Sinclair set about writing his first novel, his Romantic tendencies still dominated, but by the time he was attempting his fourth book, *Manassas*, in 1903, the social critic and the Socialist were beginning to emerge in him. The buried bitterness and rage he felt about his region's and his family's history—the issues of slavery, the Civil War, his father's illness and failure—found justification and release through the teachings of Socialism. He concluded that no one person or group is responsible for suffering and evil; natural human greed and the system of capitalism that greed has created are to blame. As he was being converted to the doctrines of Socialism, Sinclair began to take aim at the hearts and minds of his readers in order to awaken Americans so that they might reject the corruption of the present and embrace a vision of a Socialist utopia.

The 1890s and early 1900s were a remarkable period of social revolution in America. Strikes, riots, and the founding of labor unions and new political parties were frequent occurrences across the land. Four decades of a government policy of *laissez faire* toward industry had enabled corporate leaders, often called the "Robber Barons," to consolidate their power into several "trusts." Without competition, these giant monopolies were able to exploit every opportunity to make greater fortunes regardless of the human consequences. In newspapers and in fiction, several writers, labeled "muckrakers" by President Theodore Roosevelt, attempted to expose the corruption in business and government that supported the economic system. One exposé, the "embalmed beef scandal," had the support of the former Spanish-

American War hero Roosevelt himself, who testified before a Senate committee that he and his soldiers found the canned rations provided by the army to be inedible. Still, because of the powerful meat industry lobby, a bill to enforce meat inspection standards and protect consumers was dying in Congress in 1905 when the socialist weekly, *The Appeal to Reason* commissioned Sinclair to investigate the Chicago meat packing industry.

By dressing in ragged clothing and carrying a worker's pail, Sinclair spent seven weeks infiltrating the Chicago plants and neighborhoods. He then took his notes to Princeton, New Jersey, where he built a "board cabin, eight feet by ten" in which he spent nine months composing *The Jungle*. The experience involved a profound professional and personal conversion of which he later said: "I wrote with tears and anguish, pouring into the pages all the pain that life had meant to me. Externally, the story had to do with a family of stockyard workers, but internally it was the story of my own family." In the process of writing this novel, the fragments of Sinclair's intellectual life—the Romantic, the reformer, the artist—found a single purpose and direction, and the writing possesses enormous energy and sustained rhetorical power. Not since Harriet Beecher Stowe's *Uncle Tom's Cabin* had there been a book that would affect such a large part of the American people and move them to action.

As the chapters appeared serially in *The Appeal*, its reputation spread outside the weekly's proletariate readership. Still, at least five established publishers rejected the book manuscript at first because of their fear of the power of the Meat Trust. Sinclair then wrote a letter to the readers of *The Appeal* asking for pre-paid orders so that the weekly might publish it in book form. When he received twelve thousand orders, Doubleday, Page and Company decided that the potential profits were worth the risk of offending the meat companies. To protect themselves, however, they insisted upon sending their editor Isaac F. Marcosson to Chicago to check Sinclair's facts. In horror, he reported "I was able to see with my own eyes much that Sinclair had never even heard about." When the novel appeared in January, 1906, it created a sensation. President Roosevelt reportedly threw his breakfast sausages out his window and called upon Sinclair to visit the White House. In spite of desperate denials by the meat industry, within six months the Pure Food and Drug Act and the Beef Inspection Act were passed.

As a piece of immediate propaganda, *The Jungle* struck a target effectively, and it had made its author world famous as well. Sinclair would go on to publish scores of books that would be translated into over fifty languages, he would be nominated for the Nobel Prize by a committee of leading intellectuals including Albert Einstein, and he would eventually move to California and nearly win election as Governor in 1934. But as a lifelong reformer and Socialist until his death in 1968 at the age of ninety, Sinclair regretted that his most important book had not achieved the goal he had intended, for his goal was more ambitious than to sicken the American people with images of diseased and filthy meat and thereby reform one industry.

From the time of his conversion to Socialism, Upton Sinclair yearned to educate the public about the larger evils of an economic and social system that destroyed millions of lives every year through disease, poverty, and mental torture. He sought to expose the great lie of the American Dream, of freedom and opportunity for all, and to generate a revolution in the hearts and minds of Americans that would usher in a truly utopian society that would fulfill the promise of prosperity for each and every citizen. When he campaigned for Governor, he did so on the EPIC platform, which stood for "End Poverty in California." In politics, he came closer to achieving his larger goals, and only a vigorous and costly effort by California business groups barely prevented his victory.

In most discussions of *The Jungle*, the question that troubled Sinclair himself continues to be central—if it could have such a spectacular effect upon food and drug reform, why didn't this book inspire more general social upheaval? Historians and social scientists attribute *The Jungle*'s failure to achieve more comprehensive social reforms to Sinclair's simplistic images of life in the stockyard neighborhood he called Packing-town. They argue that Sinclair's picture is too one-sided to be really convincing: that many workers were actually able to create decent home lives; that the union was able to raise the living standards through strikes and negotiations; that housing and living conditions were not as dreadful as he depicted; and that the religious faith and endurance of many immi-grant workers enabled them to survive and provide opportunities for their children to gain educations and escape the conditions of poverty. Sinclair's working class readers might well have been revolted by the images of poisoned rats and tubercular animals ground into sausages, but they could not let themselves identify with the fate of the Rudkus family and the novel's strident appeals for Socialism.

Some of the Sinclair's critics argue that the workers' desire to succeed in the face of economic and physical hardships had to cause Sinclair's readers to reject the notion that the workers were only "cogs in the wheels of a machine" or "rats in a trap." In spite of all the evidence to the contrary in books and in daily life, poor immigrants kept clinging to the hopes contained for them in the word "America." From the point of view of social science then, the reason that Sinclair could only hit the stomachs of his readers instead of their hearts was that their hearts had already been shielded by myths of America against the ultimate argument of his book that salvation could only come through the nation's turning to Socialism. Still historians include the book in their courses on the period because it does provide important insights into many aspects of the politics and social history of the early twentieth century.

When literary critics attempt to assess Sinclair's achievement as a novelist in *The Jungle*, another set of issues comes to the fore. From the time of its publication, critics have compared the work to those of the great nineteenth century European and American novelists, such as Dickens, Tolstoy, and Zola, as well as to some of Sinclair's American contemporaries, Frank Norris and Theodore Dreiser. Admirers of the novel point to its rapidly developing plot, the vivid descriptions of the physical conditions of the city and the factories, and the journalistic reporting of the details of the practical financial problems of workers as they attempt to respond to the capricious speedups and slowdowns and layoffs at the companies.

Some of the most admired passages in the novel are ones that Sinclair handled with subtlety, such as the Rudkus family's gradual realization that hidden costs of insurance and interest in their homeowner's contract would inevitably cause them to lose their house and thereby waste all the brutal labor they invested in it. As a neighbor questions them about their payments, the terrifying reality of their situation becomes evident:

> "You say twelve dollars a month; but that does not include the interest."
>
> Then they stared at her. "Interest!" they cried.
>
> "But we don't have to pay any interest!" they exclaimed, three or four at once. "We only have to pay twelve dollars each month."
>
> And for this she laughed at them. "You are like all the rest," she said, "they trick you and eat you alive."
>
> . . . Then, with a horrible sinking of the heart, Teta Elzvieta unlocked her bureau and brought out the paper that had already caused them so many agonies. Now they sat around, scarcely breathing, while the old lady, who could read English, ran over it. "Yes," she said, finally, "here it is, of course: 'With interest thereon monthly, at the rate of seven percent per annum.'"
>
> And there followed a dead silence. "What does that mean?" asked Jurgis finally, almost in a whisper.
>
> "That means," replied the other, "that you have to pay them seven dollars next month, as well as the twelve dollars."
>
> "Then again there was not a sound. It was sickening, like a nightmare, in which suddenly something gives way beneath you, and you feel yourself sinking, sinking, down into bottomless abysses. As if in a flash of lightning they saw themselves—victims of a relentless fate, cornered, trapped, in the grip of destruction."

After expressing more agony as they realize that their combined meager salaries would not be sufficient to meet the house payments and also provide other necessities, Jurgis resorts to his usual "I will work harder," but they all know that like many others before them they would sacrifice everything to meet the payments only to lose everything in the end, which they do.

In such episodes, Sinclair appears to have genuine understanding of the plight of his subjects and to be able to make their predicament real for the reader. At the same time, his work has been strongly criticized for lacking fully human characters, for being an allegory in which the main character Jurgis is Everyman on a journey through a fantastic and unbelievable series of tragedies that could never happen to a single person. Sinclair has also been berated for not learning about the culture of the Lithuanian immigrants and accused of creating mechanical stereotypical characters about whom it is difficult for readers to care. And it must be acknowledged that Sinclair's fervor and eagerness to convey his message of a Socialist solution led him to extremes in some sections of the novel, especially the preachy final pages.

In his depictions of the ruthless and almost inhuman strikebreakers who both lived and worked in the meat plants to avoid encountering the striking workers outside, Sinclair seems to forget his sympathies for the poor as well as his concern for Black Americans that he had expressed in an earlier novel, *Manassas*. Insensitive and racist are the only terms to describe such passages as this:

> "One might see . . . young white girls from the country rubbing elbows with big buck Negroes with daggers in their boots, while rows of woolly heads peered down from every window of the surrounding factories. The ancestors of these people had been savages in Africa; and since then they had been chattel slaves, or had been held down by a community ruled by the traditions of slavery. Now for the first time they were free—free to gratify every passion, free to wreck themselves. . . . They lodged men and women on the same floor; and with the night there began a saturnalia of debauchery—scenes such as never before had been witnessed in America. As the women were the dregs from the brothels of Chicago, and the men were for the most part ignorant country Negroes, the nameless diseases of vice were soon rife; and this where food was being handled which was sent out to every corner of the civilized world."

While it is evident that in the tradition of Harriet Beecher Stowe's *Uncle Tom's Cabin,* Sinclair is desperately trying here to evoke America's sympathy for the striking workers by arousing the moral outrage of his readers, his blatant racism demonstrates his tendency to forget the particular human beings he is representing when he is focused upon a political issue. Not only do these passages reflect Sinclair's own prejudices, they also demonstrate the racist attitudes in the society to which Sinclair's images are a shameful attempt to appeal. No issue would arouse the public to urge the companies to bargain with the unions more effectively than that of young African-American men taking the factory jobs of whites, sleeping with white women, and learning the pleasures of debauchery.

As many literary critics have noted, Sinclair was not trying to produce a great work of art; he was trying to convert his society to Socialism. To that end he used every rhetorical and literary device he had learned from his own hack writing of juvenile stories, from the methods of romantic and senti-mental fiction, and from the major and minor propagandists in fiction who preceded him. The breakdowns in style, a clumsy narrator-visitor who medi-ates between the reader and the characters, the awkward shifts and some-times unbelievable developments in the story, and the often cardboard and stereotypical characterizations, such as that of the callous, greedy midwife who presides at the deaths of Ona and her baby—these and other flaws have been evident to readers from the start. What is remarkable in view of these deficiencies is the amazing success Sinclair achieved seventy-five years ago and the continued power the text has for readers today.

Accounting for the power and achievement of *The Jungle* has always proven a more difficult task for critics than assessing its weaknesses. Why can the events and people depicted still move readers to tears today? Perhaps it is that for all of his descriptions of horrifying physical pain and suffering, the text never loses sight of the psychological anguish that Jurgis and Ona endure: the humiliation, the guilt, the embarrassment, and the genuine despair into which they finally slide after starting out with such hope, eager-ness, and the willingness to work to exhaustion just to achieve a bit of happi-ness. One of the most compelling sequences in the book occurs when Jurgis is arrested for the first time for assaulting a boss who has corrupted Ona by threatening to prevent the entire family from getting work unless she sleeps with him. Sinclair provides a moving account of Jurgis' slow realization of his plight; as he sits helplessly in the jail, he foresees the impact his confinement will likely have upon the entire family. Because of his passionate act of revenge, those left at home will be unable to pay the rent, they will lose the house, Ona will have the child and may die for lack of medical care, and they will all be reduced to the lowest point of existence: "And they would lose it all; they would be turned out into the streets, and have to hide in some icy garret, and live or die as best they could! Jurgis had all night—and all of many more nights—to think about this, and he saw the thing in its details; he lived it all, as if he were there." Anyone who has ever committed a rash act in a moment of passion and then reflected upon the string of consequences they have set in motion and are unable stop can identify with Jurgis' hand-wringing agony.

Throughout the work, Sinclair depicts the mental lives of the workers, especially of Jurgis and Ona, vividly enough that readers in all jobs and social classes can identify with their inner tortures, even though the external events of the characters' lives may sometimes seem farfetched. It might be argued that this particular strength of the novel is a consequence of the same dimension of Sinclair's artistic approach that leads to some of the book's weaknesses. That is, Sinclair himself had been poor but was not of the working class, and he was always looking at the lives of his Packingtown people from the outside—at a distance. Thus, perhaps the only way that he could bridge the gap between his own life and theirs was by focusing upon the more universal anguish of mind accompanying the destructive physical sufferings and losses.

Sinclair claims that when he had finished his research, he was not sure of how he could begin this book. On his last night in Chicago, he happened upon a Lithuanian wedding party to which all passersby were welcomed. He sat watching the festivities for hours, rapidly taking notes. What became apparent throughout the festivities was the combination of joy and anguish that the wedding celebration contained for the newlyweds; the anguish stemmed from the failure of the guests to contribute enough money to cover the cost of the festivities; this meant that the couple would start their lives together heavily in debt. For Sinclair, the event captured the terrible ironies and disappointments which he had seen repeated during his seven weeks at the stockyards. That image of the wedding became the opening chapter of *The Jungle*, and in our first encounter with the innocent Ona and the indomitable Jurgis, we see them move from a few hours of pleasure and joy to a renewed panic over their deepening poverty. As the crowd "at the expense of the host drink themselves sodden," Ona and Jurgis watch the bills climb: "the family was helpless with dismay. So long they had toiled, and such an outlay they had made! Ona stood by, her eyes wide with terror. Those frightful bills—how they haunted her, each item gnawing at her soul all day and spoiling her rest at night."

For all of his vivid pictures of vermin, putrefaction, horrible injuries, and physical pain, Sinclair's genius as a writer was in his awareness that it is the lack of hope for the future, the mental anguish and despair that separate the people from the suffering animals that surrounded them in Packingtown. As long as poverty exists, the force of its frustrations and hopelessness will torment and crush the souls of many who endure it. The depiction of this tragic process gives *The Jungle* its lasting appeal and was Sinclair's best argument for his doctrines of Socialism.

JACQUELINE TAVERNIER-COURBIN

The Call of the Wild *and* The Jungle:
Jack London's and Upton Sinclair's Animal and Human Jungles

$\mathbf{B}$oth leading American realists, both dedicated and militant socialists, Jack London and Upton Sinclair were nevertheless completely different in temperament and philosophy of life. Although they appreciated each other's works, they only met twice, in circumstances not entirely favorable for the development of a friendship. Whereas London hailed the publication of Sinclair's *The Jungle* with generous praise, thus propelling the book and its author toward international fame, Sinclair was less generous in his appraisal of London, basing his criticism not on the work but on the man. Voicing his own deep-set puritanical nature, he damned London for such sins as smoking, drinking, enjoying sex, resigning from the Socialist party, and making too much money. As Charmian London commented, Sinclair's misapprehensions were partly due to his lack of personal acquaintance with London and to his never having seen him sober, both their meetings having taken place in New York where London was seldom on his best behavior. It is unfortunate that Sinclair did not accept London's invitation to visit him at his Glen Ellen ranch in California, since it would have been his only opportunity to see him at work, sober in his own surroundings. But London's invitation was expressed in his typically direct way, a language which Sinclair found easy to misinterpret:

From *The Cambridge Companion to American Realism and Naturalism.* © 1995 by Cambridge University Press.

Why not plan for you and your wife to run up and visit us at this time. It is a dandy place to work; if you wish you can stay in your own room and have your meals sent in to you and work twenty-four hours out of the twenty-four. . . .

You and I ought to have some "straight from the shoulder" talk with each other. It is coming to you, it may be coming to me. It may illuminate one or the other or both of us.

Sinclair refused London's invitation because George Sterling had told him that Jack had become rude, domineering, and would allow no one to argue with him. Sinclair was perhaps unaware that Sterling was a lively and inventive gossip who resented Jack and Charmian's withdrawal from the close companionship they shared for a long time, and who gossiped to London about his visits with the Sinclairs:

I've just put in a week with the Sinclairs . . . where I walked, chopped wood and gathered apples and nuts ad lib., about paying for my keep, I guess.

Upton is something fierce, but his wife is adorable. He'd not let me whistle in the house, and if I left a door open he felt the draft and put up a howl.

Although both Sinclair and London rebelled at man's cruelty and felt deeply for the downtrodden and the poor, they were never friends and went about improving the world in different ways. Disappointed by the Socialist party's inaction and the mediocrity of its leaders, and convinced that it would go nowhere because Americans prefer democratic to revolutionary methods, London felt that he could reach more people through his work than through political action and devoted his considerable energies to his writing and to developing and improving his ranch, striving to restore the land to its former richness before the destructive advent of the American pioneer. The betterment of agricultural conditions was his other social dream, and he became one of the first dedicated environmentalists. Sinclair, on the other hand, remained politically active into his sixties.

Both writers were effective muckrakers, but London always subordinated that activity to the novelist's craft, whereas Sinclair did the opposite. London's propagandistic works include didactic sociological essays; a book-length report of his firsthand observations in the East End of London, *The People of the Abyss;* and fictional works which both exposed social injustice and cruelty and aimed at reform, such as *The Star Rover* which revealed the horrors of the straitjacket in American prisons and was instrumental in bringing about the abrogation of the law allowing its use in 1913. However, neither his storytelling not his character development suffered from London's desire to arouse public awareness. Indeed, while much of his fiction is the vehicle for a message, the message is seldom an assault upon the reader. Novels such as *Martin Eden* and *The Sea Wolf*, intended as pleas against individualism, were interpreted as exalting it, which depressed and angered London. Nonetheless, this misunderstanding was an indirect and unwitting tribute to his talent, for both are powerful novels dramatizing such lifelike protagonists that the message gets lost. Martin Eden and Wolf Larsen embody individualism with such passion, intelligence, romance, and lust for life that one cannot but identify with them.

The immediate success of *The Call of the Wild*, which catapulted London onto the international scene, and the praise lavished upon it by critics, surprised London, who knew that the book was different from other dog stories but was unaware that he had written a brilliant human allegory. Begun as a normal dog story meant to redeem the species from a previous story, "Bâtard," which had dramatized a dog-made-devil by a sadistic master, *The Call of the Wild* "got away" from London and turned out to be far more of "a shot in the dark" then he could possibly have imagined. What he did realize clearly, however, was the therapeutic value of writing the book. Sitting down to it soon after his return from England in 1902, he indirectly expressed his violent reaction against the human jungle he had know in the East End of London; life in a natural jungle seemed an enviable situation by contrast.

Like other American realists of the late nineteenth century, both London and, to a lesser extent, Sinclair were influenced by Emile Zola, and both *The Call of the Wild* and *The Jungle* share characteristics of the naturalistic novel as defined in *The Experimental Novel*. Interest in contemporary French literature was a striking feature of cultural life in the United States during the last decade of the nineteenth century, and Zola's popularity is evidenced by the numerous translations of his works and by the fact that even novels he had not written were published under his name. But American publishers exploited to the utmost the deeply rooted Puritan idea that French literature is essentially wicked, turning Zola's terse titles into melodramatic ones. London had twenty-two of Zola's novels in his personal library, with dates of publication ranging back to the 1880s. He was apparently reading *Germinal* as early as his oyster-pirating days on the sloop *Reindeer*, and he mentions Zola both in *A Son of the Sun* and in *Mutiny on the Elsinore*. He also owned numerous books by other French and American realists, but it is unclear whether he had read *The Experimental Novel*, which became available in English in 1893, as he seems not to mention it anywhere. However, it is clear that his conception of fiction coincided closely with Zola's.

Like Zola, who wanted the naturalistic novel to be a documentary work based solidly on physical reality, London took the gathering of documentary evidence seriously and would go to great lengths to gather data for a story. Wanting to write an American version of his own *People of the Abyss*, he intended to find "some hell-hole of a prison, and have [himself] arrested and sent to it." While he was researching the book, he lived for seven weeks the life of the poorest among the workers and vagrants in the East End of London. He slept and ate in sordid hellholes where people had to wait in line for six or more hours before being admitted, where bunks were slept in continuously in shifts of eight hours, and where one had to break twelve hundred pounds of stone or empty the garbage of hospitals, thus being exposed to contagious diseases, to pay for a night's filthy bed. He saw the ugliest aspects of death and the most miserable ones. After seven weeks of such a life, London emerged from the East End scarred but with a well-documented book which is a violent indictment of a society which allows men to be reduced to a level of existence below that of animals. Before undertaking a new story, London would also carefully research his topic, collecting newspaper clippings and articles, magazines and books, and keeping files for future use on every topic of interest. For instance, over fifteen years, he accumulated a file containing twenty-eight newspaper articles on prison life which he used in writing *The Star Rover*, thus supplementing Ed Morrell's personal memories of San Quentin with other factual data. Indeed, although, at times, it deals with science fiction and astral projection, London's fiction is firmly grounded in reality and based on human documents, usually satisfying the requirements of logic and known scientific data.

Influenced in particular by his reading of Darwin and Spencer, London believed in evolution and determinism, the influence of heredity and of the milieu, as evidenced by much of his work and the abundant notes he left behind. But these beliefs were tempered by a deep love of humanity and a loathing for the cruelty that often characterizes man's treatment of animals and other men. London's accurate descriptions of the inhumanity of man is not a gloating over blood and knuckles, as so many critics have claimed, but an expression of his abhorrence of cruelty and his belief that the best way to expose it is to describe it unemotionally and accurately. Indeed, both Zola and London believed that the novel should neither preach nor satirize but only dramatize life objectively, never drawing conclusions, because the conclusions are implicit in the material. Both also intended the novel to be a powerful social tool but felt that an accurate and objective picture of society and mankind, presented with clinical detachment, is more effective than a compassionate dramatization of man's misery. London made his point clear in a vibrant defense of Kipling's methods and the apparent heartlessness of his descriptions—"The color of tragedy is red. Must the artist also paint the watery tears and wan-faced grief?"—and in his review of Maxim Gorky's *Foma Gordyeeff*:

> One lays the book down sick at heart—sick for life with all its "lyings and its lusts." But it is a healthy book. So fearful is its portrayal of social disease, so ruthless its stripping of the painted charm from vice, that its tendency cannot but be strongly for good. It is a goad, to prick sleeping human consciences awake and drive them into the battle for humanity.

Much like other American realists, however, London had problems with Zola's credo which held that morality should be no more relevant to literature than to science. London was no prude, but he well knew that American readers would not tolerate a frank portrayal of love from an American writer. Although he suggests passionate love in his stories and novels, he never describes it as such, and it only manifests itself in its results: the extent of the lover's sacrifices for the loved one. But he never describes physical contact between human beings in any detail.

The Call of the Wild does not dramatize directly the social problems of the day but focuses on the 1897 Gold Rush, including a vivid portrayal of Klondike types as embodied by the four sets of masters who in turn own Buck: initially, the essentially fair and efficient government couriers François and Perrault, and later the "Scotch half-breed" in charge of the mail train, who along with the other drivers is also just, despite harsh circumstances, and who respects the dogs and spares them what suffering he can. The last two sets of masters Buck works under are dramatically opposite: first, the self-indulgent, ignorant, greedy, and hypocritical Mercedes, Charles, and Hal, who have no respect for the dogs and are made to stand for the worst of the "chekakos"; then John Thornton, the ideal master, "[who] saw to the welfare of his [dogs] as if they were his own children, because he could not help it." Clearly, London cannot dramatize through the eyes of a dog all, or even most, of the social reality of a Klondike invaded by a quarter-million gold hunters, of whom only a scant fifty thousand made it to Dawson City and the North. What he could do was make the human characters he portrayed widely representative Klondike types he knew and had heard of—types who recur frequently in his other stories of the North.

London's documentation was extensive, as he spent the best part of a year taking part in the Gold Rush, leaving San Francisco on 25 July 1897 and eventually floating down the Yukon, scurvy-ridden, on a raft the following spring. London's party made the trip from Dyea Beach to the Stewart River, where they settled for the winter, in two months, arriving on October 9, four days before the river was traditionally supposed to freeze up, and taking possession of a cabin on an island between the mouth of the Steward River and the mouth of Henderson Creek. Jack toiled with the rest, daily increasing the load he was packing, until he was proud to pack as well as the Indians, carrying a hundred pounds to the load on good trails and seventy-five pounds on bad ones. Since his outfit weighed a thousand pounds, he carried every load for one mile and came back for the next, thus walking nineteen miles for every mile of progression if he carried ten loads, and twenty-nine miles if he carried fifteen loads. Their route took them over the Chilkoot Pass to Lake Linderman, where they constructed a boat between 9 and 21 September. Jack's skill in handling small boats allowed them to make their way through Lakes Linderman, Bennet, Tagish, and Marsh before entering Fifty Mile River, which narrowed into two dangerous rapids: Box Canyon and White Horse rapids. The river trip from Lake Linderman took them a little less than three weeks, and they decided to make camp on Upper Island, a wise choice, as Dawson was crowded and there was the threat of food shortage.

After staking eight claims, they made their way downriver by boat to Dawson where London spent six weeks, during which he observed the gold city. It was on 5 November, the day Dawson woke to find the Yukon frozen, that London filed his claim at the gold-records office for his gold strike on Henderson Creek, eighteen days after he first arrived in the city. London spent a great deal of time in Dawson's saloons during these few weeks, often in conversation with some veteran sourdough or noted town character. It was also in such bars that sourdoughs were famous for gambling away their fortunes. If *The Call of the Wild* contains only two saloon scenes (the scene at Circle City in which Buck attacks "Black Burton" and the one in the Eldorado Saloon in Dawson as a result of which Buck is made to pull a sled loaded with a thousand pounds of flour), many of London's stories of the North dramatize the drinking, talking, gambling, and dancing he had witnessed and the places, saloons, restaurants, Opera House, or commercial stores he had frequented. The only aspect of life he avoided describing was prostitution, which was rampant. In fact, dance-hall girls are always treated kindly and gallantly in London's Klondike fiction, often dramatized as kinder human beings than their more respectable sisters: "Butterflies, bits of light and song and laughter, dancing, dancing down the last tail-reach of hell."

Those weeks in Dawson netted London many tales, and the raw frontier town appears often in his stories; but it was during the winter in camp that he came to know the Alaska of the sourdoughs and Indians. Aside from reading *The Origin of Species* and Milton's *Paradise Lost*, which he had taken with him up north, and swapping books with his companions, London's favorite recreation was talking and arguing. Eagerly he questioned the old-timers, listening avidly to their adventures until a picture of Alaska in trail-breaking days grew in his mind. The camp offered a cross-section of the new life that was pulsating through the North. Among the men who most impressed London was Louis Savard, a generally silent French Canadian who provided the inspiration for Louis Savoy in *The Son of the Wolf* and for characteristics of both François and Perrault in *The Call of the Wild*, while Nig, Louis's lovable sled dog who cleverly evaded work, probably became "That Spot" and, according to Joan London, one of Buck's companions. Emil Jensen, who was fifteen years older than London, and whom London greatly admired, became the model for Malemute Kid, London's central and idealized figure in *The Son of the Wolf* and *The God of His Fathers*, as well as for John Thornton.

How much personal experience London had with Northland dogs is difficult to determine. There were many dogs around, and he probably saw some of the best husky teams in the area, as the main trail ran near his cabin, and witnessed more than one prize dog put through the test of breaking a heavily laden sled out of the ice. He also knew well two "outsiders"— Newfoundlands and Saint Bernards—who learned to hold their own on Split-up Island: Louis Savard's Nig and especially Louis Bond's Jack, a cross between a Saint Bernard and Scotch Collie, whom London greatly admired and whose qualities he used in Buck's characterization:

> Yes, Buck is based upon your dog at Dawson. And of course Judge Miller's place was Judge Bond's—even to the cement swimming tank & the artesian well. And don't you remember that your father was attending a meeting of the fruit-growers Association the night I visited you, and Louis was organizing an athletic club—all of which events figured with Buck if I remember correctly.

What information London did not have he gathered from his reading, in particular Egerton R. Young's *My Dogs in the Northland*, published late in 1902, a few months before London started writing *Call of the Wild*. He probably learned much about the handling and behavior of sled dogs from this book, and several of the dogs in the novel resemble some of Young's dogs: "Young's Jack, a St. Bernard, has some of Buck's feelings of responsibility; Cuffy, a Newfoundland, is not unlike the feminine Curly; the one-eyed husky lead dog Voyageur may have contributed to the portrayal of unsociable, one-eyed Sol-leks; the behavior of Young's Rover, who constantly licks the wounds of other dogs in the team, may have suggested the role of doctor dog assumed by Skeet." Although plagiarism would occasionally be charged against London, his use of such sources was generally a borrowing of technical data that affected neither plot, tone, theme, nor symbolism. He had visited the territory, he knew what he was describing, he had observed and experienced much, and such secondhand data was used to fill the gaps of his knowledge and provide realistic detail and a feeling of authenticity.

However, although *The Call of the Wild* is well documented, it is not crammed with factual data, for London did not believe in providing details that might detract from the "thrust and go" of his story. In his otherwise laudatory review of *The Octopus*, London complained of Norris's passion for documentary detail. As far as London was concerned, no one cared "whether Hooven's meat safe be square or oblong; whether it be lined with wire screen or mosquito netting; whether it be hung to the branches of an oak tree or to the ridgepole of the barn; whether, in fact, Hooven has a meat safe or not." Indeed, he described his own art as "idealized realism"—an art that did not shy away from reality, even in its ugliest aspects, but attempted to grasp the true romance of things at the same time—and always defended his own fiction when attacked by critics who reproached him for giving insufficient detail:

> When I have drawn a picture in a few strokes, he would spoil it by putting in the multitude of details I have left out. . . . His trouble is that he does not see with a pictorial eye. He merely looks upon a scene and sees every bit of it; but he does not see the true picture in that scene, a picture which can be thrown upon a canvas by eliminating a great mass of things that spoil the composition, that obfuscate the true beautiful lines of it.

The influence of the milieu and heredity, the concept of the survival of the fittest, and adaptation as the key to survival are of overwhelming importance in *The Call of the Wild*, which dramatizes the concept of devolution—the return of a civilized being to the primitive when his environment itself has changed from one of mellow civilization to one of brutality where the only law is eat or be eaten, kill or be killed. Until he is kidnapped, Buck lives the life of a sated aristocrat on Judge Miller's estate. His education into the harsh realities of an unprotected life begins shortly after he is abducted and endures a two-day-and-night train journey during which he is vilely treated and neither eats nor drinks. After changing hands a number of times, and in a fever of pain and rage, Buck meets the man in the red sweater, who provides the first step of his initiation into the wild: the dog breaker. Buck had never been struck with a club in his life, but again and again, with each new charge, he is brought crushingly to the ground by a vicious blow of the club. Although his rage knows no bounds and although he is a large, powerful dog, he is no match for a man who is "no slouch at dog-breakin'" and knows how to handle a club efficiently. The man in the red sweater finishes Buck off with a blow directly on the nose and a final "shrewd blow" that knocks him unconscious. Buck thus learns his first lesson: a man with a club is a master to be obeyed, though not necessarily placated. "That club was a revelation. It was his introduction to the reign of primitive law, and he met the introduction half-way." Buck, however, retains his dignity and never fawns on his masters. They are stronger then he; therefore he obeys them. Having seen a dog that would neither obey nor conciliate killed in the struggle for mastery makes the alternatives clear to him: to obey, to conciliate, or to die; and Buck is above all a survivor. He knows he is beaten, but his spirit is never broken.

Buck's next lessons takes place on Dyea beach when Curly, whom he has befriended, is killed by the huskies when she makes friendly advances to one of them. In two minutes, she is literally torn to pieces. "So that was the way. No fair play. Once down, that was the end of you. Well [Buck] would see to it that he never went down." This traumatic lesson often returns to haunt his sleep. There seems to be only one law in this new world, which both men and beasts obey—the law of club and fang—and, like Dave and Sol-leks, one has to learn to give nothing, ask for nothing, and expect nothing.

Adapting to a new environment also entails learning other lessons, not only simple lessons such as digging a sleeping hole in the snow or eating fast, but also lessons involving major moral changes. Buck learns to steal, and London makes it clear that his first theft marks him as fit to survive in the hostile Northland environment: "It marked his adaptability, his capacity to adjust himself to changing conditions, the lack of which would have meant swift and terrible death. It marked, further, the decay or going to pieces of his moral nature, a vain thing and a handicap in the ruthless struggle for existence." London comments with some irony that, while living on Judge Miller's estate, Buck would have died for a moral principle, such as the defense of the Judge's riding whip, "but [that] the completeness of his decivilization was now evidenced by his ability to flee from the defense of a moral consideration and so save his hide." Among other moral qualities Buck sheds are his sense of fair play and mercy, values reserved for gentler climates. In the northern wilds, survival is the only goal, and ruthlessness the only way to survive. Thus, Buck learns through experience and proves that he is eminently adaptable and fit. His body also adapts well to the new demands of the environment: he loses his fastidiousness, grows impervious to pain, achieves an internal as well as an external economy, making the most of whatever comes his way; his senses develop to an incredible acuteness, and forgotten instincts come to life in him.

Heredity also plays an important role in his survival:

> And not only did he learn by experience, but instincts long dead became alive again. The domesticated generations fell from him. In vague ways he remembered back to the youth of the breed, to the time the wild dogs ranged in packs through the primeval forest and killed their meat as they ran it down. It was no task for him to learn to fight with cut and slash and the quick wolf snap. In this manner had fought forgotten ancestors. They quickened the old life within him, and the old tricks which they had stamped into the heredity of the breed were his tricks. They came to him without effort or discovery, as though they had been his always.

The basic instinct which comes to life in Buck is the instinct to kill. He progrees quickly, beginning with small game, and eventually kills men. The instinct to kill is common to all predators; man himself has not completely lost it and indulges it when he goes shooting or hunting. However, for Buck, the killing is infinitely more intimate, as it is not carried out by proxy through a bullet; "He was ranging at the head of the pack, running the wild thing down, the living meat, to kill with his own teeth and wash his muzzle to the eyes in warm blood." The hunt of the snowshoe rabbit marks the awakening of Buck's desire to kill, and he immediately challenges Spitz to a fight, which he wins largely because the knowledge of ancestral fighting techniques becomes his instantly:

> As they circled about, snarling, ears laid back, keenly watchful for the advantage, the scene came to Buck with a sense of familiarity. He seemed to remember it all—the white woods, and earth, and moonlight, and the thrill of battle. . . . To Buck it was nothing new or strange, this scene of old time. It was as though it had always been, the wonted way of things.

After defeating Spitz, and while the pack closes in on his crippled enemy, "Buck stood and looked on, the successful champion, the dominant primordial beast who had made his kill and found it good." Buck has indeed come of age, and, although his education is not finished, he has proven that he is one of the fit.

Once Buck has proven himself on the hereditary and environmental levels and has reverted to instinctual patterns of behavior, his life with a new master, John Thornton, suddenly becomes more mellow, and he has an opportunity to relax his vigilance. But Buck cannot return to his old self, for he has learned only too well the lessons of the wild—that one should never forego an advantage or draw back from a fight one has started, that mercy is misunderstood for fear or weakness, and that such misunderstanding may lead to death. He has gained knowledge from the depth of time, and such knowledge cannot be forgotten once it has become a conscious part of the self. Thus, life with John Thornton, which could, in other circumstances, have heralded a return to the tame, is merely an interval in Buck's evolution, and the call of the wild keeps on summoning him until he has returned fully to the life of his ancestors and become a part of nature.

In the last stages of Buck's devolution, London's handling of the theme of heredity becomes increasingly mythical and archetypal. London understood clearly that Buck's progress in adapting to his environment was in fact a regression into his instinctive past, what Jung would call his "collective unconscious":

> His development (or retrogression) was rapid. . . . And when, on the still, cold nights, he pointed his nose at a star and howled long and wolflike, it was his ancestors, dead and dust, pointing nose at star and howling down through the centuries and through him. And his cadences were their cadences, the cadences which voiced their woes and what to them was the meaning of the stillness, and the cold, and the dark.

Clearly, London could not have been aware of the extent to which his dramatization of Buck's return to the wild exemplifies C. G. Jung's theories of the unconscious. Nevertheless, Buck offers a perfect harmonization of Jung's progression and regression principles. Because he must adapt to a primitive environment, the hard-won values of the conscious and the vitality and power of the unconscious are no longer at war, and adaptation to his environment involves adopting a new set of values, which enhances rather than thwarts the vitality of his unconscious.

It is the emergence of his collective unconscious added to his physical power and intelligence which allows Buck to survive. This collective unconscious warns him of danger and gives him the tools and techniques necessary to defeat his adversaries. His instant recognition of what might be a trap is a clear instance of behavior controlled by instinctive knowledge arising from the collective unconscious:

> The snow walls pressed him on every side, and a great surge of fear swept through him—the fear of the wild thing for the trap. It was a token that he was harking back through his own life to the lives of his forebears; for he was a civilized dog, an unduly civilized dog, and of his own experience knew no trap and so could not of himself fear it.

Buck's newly discovered ability to bide his time "with a patience that [is] nothing less than primitive" is also evidence of his collective unconscious, and is characteristic of predators whose only hope to eat and survive resides in their ability to lie in wait until their potential victim or foe is at a disadvantage and vulnerable to attack.

Throughout most of the book, Buck's persona and shadow are in equilibrium. He fulfills a social role where work is all-important, and, at the same time, he is in tune with his instincts. Indeed, he is now more fully alive than he ever was on Judge Miller's ranch:

> There is an ecstasy that marks the summit of life, and beyond which life cannot rise. And such is the paradox of living, this ecstasy comes when one is most alive, and it comes as a complete forgetfulness that one is alive. . . . and it came to Buck, leading the pack, sounding the wolf cry, straining after the food that was alive and that fled before him through the moonlight. He was sounding the deeps of his nature, and of the parts of his nature that were deeper than he, going back into the womb of Time. He was mastered by the sheer surging of life, the tidal wave of being, the perfect joy of each separate muscle, joint, and sinew in that it was everything that was not death, that it was aglow and rampant, expressing itself in movement, flying exultantly under the stars and over the face of dead matter that did not move.

Buck had lived a life of quiet happiness in California, which was ruled by his civilized, good-dog persona. In the Northland, after his shadow has been awakened, he lives intensely every aspect of life, be it pain, joy, love, hatred, or work. In fact, he discovers passion, which is a manifestation of the shadow.

The third stage of Buck's evolution consists in the shedding of his new sled-dog persona to adopt a third and final one: a mythical or archetypal persona that becomes the very embodiment of his shadow, as his earlier dog-persona recedes into his personal unconscious. As the "blood longing" grows stronger in him, Buck fights larger and larger prey and begins more and more to resemble his wild brothers, transforming himself in the secrecy of the forest into a thing of the wild, "stealing along softly, cat-footed, a passing shadow that appeared and disappeared among the shadows." Buck kills a large black bear and a huge bull-moose which he stalks and worries for four days before finally pulling him down, with the "dogged, tireless, persistent" patience of the wild "when it hunts its living food." Then, out of despair and anger over the murder of John Thornton, Buck attacks and kills men—the Yeehats who have massacred Thornton's party—kills them in spite of the law of club and fang. His last ties with mankind broken, Buck is now free to join and lead a pack of wolves and live the life of the wild to the fullest, thus becoming the very embodiment of his shadow, as well as a God-image symbolizing the perfect integration of the self: "When the long winter nights come on and wolves follow their meat into the lower valleys, he may be seen running at the head of the pack through the pale moonlight or glimmering borealis, leaping gigantic above his fellows, his great throat a-bellow as he sings a song of the younger world, which is the song of the pack."

From the standpoints of objectivity, amorality, and rejection of social taboos, *The Call of the Wild* is naturalistic by default, for Buck's gorgeous coat of fur allowed London to deal uninhibitedly with themes he would otherwise have shunned. Indeed, many painful and shocking scenes are described objectively. The potentially heart-rending scene in which Buck is beaten by the man in the red sweater is rendered in detail but with no expression of sympathy or pity. London does not dwell on Buck's pain, but merely describes accurately what the man does to him and how Buck reacts. The fight between Buck and Spitz, the stalking and killing of the bull-moose, and Buck's standing off the wolf pack are all scenes which London handles unemotionally, never indulging in expressions of horror or pity. He even indicates with remarkable simplicity the economy-of-pain principle upon which the moose herd functions: "it was not the life of the herd, or of the young bulls, that was threatened. The life of only one member was demanded, which was a remoter interest in their lives, and in the end they were content to pay the toll." Pain, suffering, death, London can describe objectively. Love is another matter; but, again, Buck's furry nature frees London from having to wax romantic. Although he describes Buck's passionate devotion to John Thornton in abstract terms, he never allows Buck to lose his dignity and fawn upon his master as the other dogs do. The various instances when Buck proves his love for his master, whether by attempting to jump over a chasm (which would have led to certain death), by attacking Black Burton, by risking his own life repeatedly in the rapids to save Thornton's, or by pulling a sleigh loaded with a thousand pounds of flour, are always described with great economy of emotion. London merely describes Buck's actions—love in action, not as an emotion. What expression of feeling London does dramatize is on Thornton's part. Indeed, the men are awed by the lengths to which Buck will carry his devotion, and Thornton is the one who expresses his love for Buck after the latter has won his bet for him.

The amoral stance of the novel was an easy one for London to assume, because the perfect logic of Buck's reversion to the wild is easily acceptable in an animal. It would be more difficult to accept in a human being, especially by London's early-twentieth-century audience. Many of the themes London dramatized easily in *The Call of the Wild* are present but transformed in his other fiction, where he never condones loss of moral principles for his two-legged characters. In fact, in his stories of the North, human survival demands virtues such as courage, integrity, and brotherhood. Like dogs, men must change both physically and morally, as only the strong survive; but they must change for the better morally as well as physically, substituting "unselfishness, forbearance, and tolerance" for the courtesies of ordinary life. Those who fail usually die a useless and shameful death after having lived without dignity, such as the protagonists of "In a Far Country" and the miserably incompetent Mercedes, Hal, and Charles in *The Call of the Wild*, who neither "toil hard, suffer sore, [nor] remain sweet of speech and kindly," and who embody the antithesis of what man should be in the northern wilderness. Unlike Buck, London's ideal heroes, such as Malemute Kid and John Thornton, have not lost their moral nature.

Despite this basic difference between London's dramatization of men and animals, many scenes in *The Call of the Wild* have their parallels in his other fiction of the North. Buck's blood lust and the enjoyment he experiences in fighting a worthy opponent is paralleled, for instance, by Scruff Mackenzie's fight in "The Son of the Wolf": "At first he felt compassion for his enemy; but this fled before the primal instinct of life, which in turn gave way to the lust of slaughter. The ten thousand years of culture fell from him, and he was a cave-dweller, doing battle for his female." Buck's stalking of the bull-moose, and the way he prevents the poor animal from getting food, drink, or rest, reminds one of Thomas Stevens's victimization of the mammoth in "A Relic of the Pliocene," and of the more gripping "Law of Life" and "Love of Life." For both men and dogs, imagination can make for survival when all else is equal: it allows Buck to win his fight with Spitz, when both dogs are equally matched; and the lack of it causes the death of the man in "To Build a Fire." Patience and imagination have nothing to do with great physical strength or moral character; but for both men and dogs their absence often leads to death. Indeed, in London's northern wilderness, a man's world and a dog's world have much in common, and both are ruled by naturalistic laws; but in the "dog stories" London could go further, for he was not hindered by the moral requirements of his audience, and perhaps of his own nature. He could never quite handle human protagonists with the same amoral, objective stance.

That Sir Arthur Conan Doyle should have called Upton Sinclair the "Zola of America" is ironic, as no American realist of the time was further removed from Zola's conception of fiction. Sinclair, in fact, glibly dismissed the importance of Zola's work and indeed that of all the great French writers. After beginning an elementary course in French at Columbia University with a class of freshmen and sophomores, and staying long enough to "get the pronunciation and the elements of grammar," he felt that in six weeks he could read French with reasonable fluency and read, presumably in the original, all the classics known to Americans: "all of Corneille, Racine and Molière; some of Rousseau and Voltaire; a sampling of Bossuet and Chateaubriand; the whole of Musset and Daudet, Hugo and Flaubert; about half of Balzac and Zola, and enough of Maupassant and Gautier *to be thankful that [he] had not come upon this kind of literature until [he] was to some extent mature, with a good hard shell of Puritanism to protect [him] against the black magic of the modern Babylon.*" Despite Sinclair's self-proclaimed genius, one cannot but wonder how much of this writing he understood, given his skimpy knowledge of the language. Moreover, his own deep-set puritan prejudices and his neuroticism colored his reading of every author, French or other, and accounts for his complete and self-congratulatory dismissal of a major body of great world classics on moralistic grounds.

Published three years after *The People of the Abyss* and clearly influenced by London's earlier reporting, *The Jungle* documents in fictional form the revolting conditions of work and life in Chicago's meat-packing industry. Unfortunately, in this as well as many of his other works, Sinclair tends to assault the reader with the message he wants to carry, subordinating plot, character development, and verisimilitude to propaganda. In Sinclair's own words, *The Jungle* was misread: he had "aimed at the public's heart, and by accident [had] hit it in the stomach." Not really accidental, the misreading was caused by the vividness of his descriptions of the stomach-turning conditions of work in the Chicago meat-packing plants, the deceitful and unsanitary practices of the meat industry as a whole, and, at the same time, by the presence of characters who are not lifelike and a plot that loses credibility in the last third of the novel. The sympathy and pity one initially experiences eventually give way to exasperation, as Sinclair manipulates his protagonist out of character for socialistic purposes.

By 1904, Sinclair had become a member of the Socialist Party of America and a reader of *The Appeal to Reason*, a weekly populistic-socialistic journal, contributing in September and October 1904 a series of three articles on an unsuccessful strike of the Chicago meat-packers. Just as John Steinbeck's "Their Blood Is Strong" provided the seed for *The Grapes of Wrath*, so these articles were largely the inspiration for *The Jungle*; and, as early as October 1904, Sinclair was proposing to London's editor, George P. Brett of Macmillan, a new novel which would "set forth the breaking of human hearts by a system which exploits the labor of men and women for profit." The project was eventually staked by Macmillan and Fred D. Warren, editor of *The Appeal*, in the amount of five hundred dollars each, and Sinclair left for Chicago.

For seven weeks Sinclair lived among the "wage slaves of the Beef Trust," sitting at night in the homes of the workers, foreign-born and native, listening to their stories, and making notes of everything. In the daytime he would wander about the yards and his friends would show him around. He was not much better dressed than the workers and found that by carrying a dinner-pail he could be inconspicuous and go anywhere. At the end of a month or more, he knew the story he meant to tell, but he had no characters until, on a Sunday afternoon, he saw a wedding party going into the back room of a saloon. He followed and watched. He also talked to many people—including lawyers, doctors, policemen, politicians, and real-estate agents—to complete his research, eating at the University Settlement to check his data against the opinions "of men and women who were giving their lives to this neighborhood."

Although Sinclair did not immerse himself in the Chicago stockyards as deeply as London had in the Klondike or the East End of London, remaining a spectator rather than a participant, he still gathered much documentation and got a feel for the life of the wage-slaves of Chicago. The information was clearly accurate; as a result of the uproar that followed the publication of the novel by Doubleday, Page and Company in 1906, President Roosevelt launched an investigation of the sanitary conditions in the Chicago meat-packing plants which essentially confirmed every abuse charged in *The Jungle*, with the exception of men's falling into vats and being rendered into pure-leaf lard. According to Sinclair, "There had been several cases, but always the packers had seen to it that the widows were returned to the old country."

Sinclair also included in the book much of his own experience with cold and poverty. Although belonging to a genteel Southern family, Sinclair's parents had never prospered and, with the passing of years, moved from cheap boardinghouses to cheaper ones, always trying to keep up appearances, and always failing. The contrasts among the social classes, which became Sinclair's favorite theme, was a reality of his early life, when he would visit well-to-do relatives: "one night [he] would be sleeping on a vermin-ridden sofa in a lodging-house, and the next night under the silken coverlets of a fashionable home." This schizophrenic upbringing took its toll on Sinclair, who desperately needed to support himself, and later his family, but had inherited too lofty a self-image to stoop to any form of menial labor to make his and the lives of those close to him more bearable. His first wife, Meta, is probably the person who suffered most from his refusal to hold a job, for she was not a natural ascetic and wanted a little beauty and joy in her life. More-over, Sinclair's asceticism was not exclusively economic, having much to do with his own puritanical fears of beauty, joy, and love, even in their most innocent forms. The scenes of hunger, illness, and cold in *The Jungle* were inspired by Sinclair's own experiences, in particular the winter of 1903, which he spent in a small, cold, drafty cabin in the New Jersey woods near Princeton while writing *Manassas* and living with his wife and baby on thirty dollars a month. Inevitably, sickness came, and Meta's troubles were diag-nosed as "womb trouble"—as Ona's would be in *The Jungle*. Like Ona, Meta bought patent medicines—which cured nothing but masked the pain with alcohol, opium, or some other stimulant—paying as much as a dollar for a bottle of "Lydia Pinkham's Vegetable Compound." Conditions were so dreadful that Meta even contemplated suicide, Sinclair's awakening one night to find her sitting in bed with a revolver in her hand. She suffered infi-nitely more from their poverty than her husband, for the choice of life-style had not been hers, and eventually their comfortless and often loveless marital life ended in divorce.

When Sinclair indicated that he had attempted in *The Jungle* to "put the contents of Shelley into the form of Zola," not realizing that his political idealism was doomed to destroy his naturalism, he could only have had in mind Zola's emphasis on detailed and accurate descriptions of the milieu. Indeed, *The Jungle* is an excellent documentary novel. The living conditions of the workers of Packingtown are mercilessly dissected. The rooming houses are appalling; when it rains, the streets become rivers full of stinking green water deep enough for a tall man to wade in up to the waist and for a two-year-old child to drown; "Bubbly Creek," an arm of the Chicago River where the packing-houses empty their drainage, is constantly in motion, "as if huge fish were feeding in it," because the grease and chemicals poured into it undergo strange transformations, and bubbles of carbonic acid rise to the surface and burst, making rings two or three feet wide. Chickens feed on it and the packers gather the surface filth to make lard. In the winter, they cut the surface ice of the creek and sell it in the city. The houses are built without sewers, the drainage of a generation sitting in cesspools beneath them. The workers are surrounded by endless vistas of ugly and dirty little wooden buildings, foul smells ("an elemental odor, raw and crude. . . . rich, almost rancid, sensual and strong,") thick, black, oily smoke, and an elemental sound made of "the distant lowing of ten thousand cattle, the distant grunting of ten thousand swine."

Not only do the workers live in a sewer of germs and bacteria, but everything they eat is adulterated: tea, coffee, sugar, flour, and milk are doctored with chemicals such as formaldehyde: sausage bought in America is not the nutritious food the emigrants had eaten a great deal of in Lithuania. Its color created by chemicals, its smoky flavor a result of more chemicals, and its contents of potato flour and spoilt meat, the stink of which has been removed by yet more chemicals, "it has no more food value than so much wood," when it is not actually lethal. Sinclair's horrifying descriptions of the processing of meat struck a responding chord in the reading public. Sympathize as they might with the plight of the workers, the thought of the unspeakable mixtures they were buying under the fancy names of "boneless hams," "California hams," "head cheese," or "smoked sausage" was a direct hit to the readers' stomachs and pocket books.

> There was never the least attention paid to what was cut up for sausage; there would come all the way back from Europe old sausage that had been rejected, and that was moldy and white— it would be dosed with borax and glycerine, and dumped into the hoppers, and made over again for home consumption. There would be meat that had tumbled out on the floor, in the dirt and sawdust, where the workers had tramped and spit countless billions of consumption germs. There would be meat stored in great piles in rooms . . . and thousands of rats would race about on it. . . . These rats were nuisances, and the packers would put poisoned bread for them; they would die, and then rats, bread, and meat would go into the hoppers together.

The processing of hams was not much better, spoilt hams being pickled and colored chemically to hide the smell and taste. Government inspectors, paid to screen hogs' carcasses for tuberculosis, would enter into conversation and let a dozen carcasses go by without feeling the glands of the neck, while explaining the deadly nature of ptomaine. The condemned meat industry was a particular horror. Inspectors were paid merely to make sure that diseased meat was kept in the state. Thus, carcasses of tubercular steers, containing deadly poison, were sold in the city. "There was said to be two thousand dollars a week hush money from the tubercular steers alone; and as much again from the hogs which had died of cholera on the trains, and which you might see any day being loaded into boxcars and hauled away to a place called Globe, in Indiana, where they made a fancy grade of lard."

> There were cattle which had been fed on "whiskey-malt," the refuse of the breweries, and had become what the men called "steerly"—which means covered with boils. It was a nasty job killing these, for when you plunged your knife into them they would burst and splash foul-smelling stuff into your face. . . . It was stuff such as this that made the "embalmed beef" that had killed several times as many United States soldiers as all the bullets of the Spaniards; only the army beef, besides, was not fresh canned, it was old stuff that had been lying for years in the cellars.

Small wonder that the miserable fate of the workers turned out to be of remoter interest to Sinclair's readers than their realization of the contaminated food they were eating, and that the public outcry following the book's publication, despite angry disclaimers on the part of the packers and a vicious press war, led directly to the passing of the Meat Inspection Bill on 26 May 1906 and of the Pure Food and Drug Bill, which had been stalled in Congress for months, in June 1906. Even after the passing of these bills, Americans did not regain their appetite for processed meat for decades.

Sinclair's descriptions of dehumanizing working conditions in the meat-packing plants are just as powerful, but met largely with reader indifference. The law of supply and demand governs everything and the workers are mercilessly exploited. If they arrive at work a minute late, they are docked an hour's pay; if they arrive several minutes late, they lost their job and have to join the hungry crowd at the packing-house's gate. When there is little work, the packers keep the workers waiting most of the day without pay in twenty degrees-below-zero temperature in the winter or sweltering heat with an overpowering stench in the summer. Then, "speeding-up" begins late in the afternoon, when the packers have bought the day's cattle on their own terms. "Speeding-up" the general practice, brings about crippling and deadly accidents, for which the packers never assume responsibility.

> On the killing beds you were apt to be covered with blood, and it would freeze solid; if you leaned against a pillar you would freeze to that, and if you put your hand upon the blade of a knife, you would run a chance of leaving your skin on it. . . . Also the air would be full of steam, from the hot water and the hot blood, so that you could not see five feet before you; and then, with men

rushing about at the speed they kept up on the killing beds, and
all with butcher knives, like razors, in their hands—well, it was to
be counted a wonder that there were not more men slaughtered
than cattle.

Sinclair's descriptions of the workers' injuries are as repulsive as those of
meat processing: pickle-room workers and wool-pluckers have their fingers
eaten off by acid one by one; butchers', boners', and trimmers' hands are
mere lumps of flesh; stamping-machine workers have parts of their hands
chopped off; fertilizer men's skins are soaked with phosphates that cannot be
washed off, killing them in a few years and making it impossible to stay close
to them without gasping.

Such descriptions are the most vital aspect of the book and remain
more vivid in the readers' minds than the characters. If heredity plays no
part in the novel, the influence of the milieu does, as no one can remain
physically and mentally immune from such misery. Alcoholism is, for many,
a natural consequence of unbearable living conditions; prostitution and
corruption often appear as the only means of survival: "nobody rose in
Packingtown by doing good work . . . if you met a man who was rising in
Packingtown, you met a knave." The poor graft off each other; votes are
bought many times over by opposing parties; police, courts of law, and city
hall are on the packers' payroll; acts of kindness are rare and come from the
lowest and poorest. Like London's Buck, Jurgis and his family learn that
this is an inimical world where one can give nothing, expect nothing, and
ask for nothing: "It was a war of each against all, and the devil take the
hindmost. You did not give feasts to other people, you waited for them to
give feasts to you. You went about with your soul full of suspicion and
hatred. You understood that you were environed by hostile powers that
were trying to get your money. . . ."

Moral integrity and traditions are the natural causalities of such an
environment, as Jurgis discovers during his wedding, when his guests do not
honor the *veselija* and leave the newlyweds to pay for the expenses of the
feast. Sentiments die from lack of expression. Indeed, it is difficult to express
tenderness when one is constantly dead tired, cold, and hungry. But jealousy
and blind rage do not die along with Jurgis's ability to express love, and,
unfortunately, these are the very emotions he cannot afford to indulge, as the
logical consequences of his attack on Connor inexorably make clear: the poor
cannot afford to live by the same moral principles as the bourgeoisie. Moral
and social rules, when not adapted to actual circumstances, become destructive. This theme, which reminds one of Stephen Crane's "Maggie: A Girl of
the Streets," where a drunken, vicious hag of a mother drives Maggie away

from their hovel of a "home" on moral principles, thereby ensuring her eventual suicide, is summarized by Marija: "When people are starving . . . and they have anything with a price, they ought to sell it, I say. I guess you realize it now when it's too late. Ona could have taken care of us all, in the beginning." Marija, who becomes a prostitute when there are no other means of survival, keeps the rest of the family alive and sends the children to school. Jurgis's moral indignation, or rather insane jealousy, brings about the death of his wife through starvation, the loss of their house, and incredible hardship for the whole family, including the death of his only son. The women in the novel seem to bow more easily to the requirements of a brutal environment, understanding, like Buck, that the defense of moral considerations has little place in the jungle. Jurgis, too, is eventually ready to relinquish his moral integrity when it serves his interest and becomes a criminal, a strike breaker, a boss taking graft, and a corrupt political agitator.

Sinclair's characters are hardly believable at times for several reasons, in particular, because he gives them a North American rather than a European mentality. In actual fact, the likelihood of a family of poor European immigrants buying a house a little more than a week after arriving in America and sinking all their savings into it against the advice of those who have more experience, when they have many mouths to feed and only some of the adults have neither secure nor well-paid jobs, is almost inconceivable. Sinclair compounds the improbability by having them take out a large mortgage on the house and buy their furniture on credit, when the very concept of credit was, to say the least, disreputable in Europe until recently, especially among the poor. Thus, the premise for plot and characterization is flawed, especially as Sinclair does not draw Jurgis as being either stupid or unconventional, but as merely stubborn. Letting women close the deal on a house purchase would also have been inconceivable for a European peasant, and even more so when he could not understand the language or read the legal documents. Such people were above all survivors, who had fought hardship for centuries and hung onto their money for dear life, suspicious of others' motivations—a fact to which Sinclair merely pays lip service: "Still, they were peasant people, and they hung on the their money by instinct." Even a reader unfamiliar with the European mentality cannot help questioning Jurgis's stubborn disregard of the advice of friends who have been in America longer than he, and the speed and gullibility with which he makes such important decisions.

Furthermore, too many catastrophes happen to Jurgis and his family to allow the reader to identify with them fully. Sinclair clearly telescoped all the woes he had witnessed in many workingmen's families into the lot of a single family, with little regard for credibility. But, because he pushed too hard, divesting his characters of resourcefulness and vitality and depriving them of control, he processed them into trapped animals or mindless cogs, thus arousing the reader's sympathy only for a time. In fact, animal and mechanical imagery abounds, none perhaps more powerful than the slaughtered hogs simile. Zola wanted characters to be individuals in their own right as well as largely representative of their social class, and he knew better than to make one single man or family bear the cross of the cumulative mistakes and pains of their group. In a humorless analog to Voltaire's *Candide, everything* goes wrong for Jurgis, and his life knows no relief or unpredictable and joyful occasions. Indeed, the true may not always be believable, and, in Frank Norris's words, fiction is what *seems* real, not what *is* real—a fact Sinclair disregarded when he decided to stack the deck of Jurgis's miseries. Even though such a relentless succession of disasters is possible in life, it is too much for a reader to accept in fiction. From the moment the family sets foot in America, they are robbed by almost everyone they encounter; when it should have provided a tidy nest-egg, the wedding feast leaves them over a hundred dollars in debt; they are thoroughly swindled in the purchase of their house, and eventually lose it and all the money they put into it; old Antanas dies of blood poisoning after saltpeter has eaten through his boots and feet; young Stanislovas is eaten alive by rats in a basement and little Antanas is drowned in the street; Marija and Jurgis lose their jobs because of accidents and because they are headstrong, and Marija eventually turns to prostitution and drugs; Ona is terrorized into prostituting herself to keep her job, loses it after Jurgis beats up her boss, then, at eighteen, dies in childbirth of starvation and cold.

When catastrophes are not brought about by fate, Jurgis brings them upon himself by willfully disregarding the advice of those who have more experience or by acting on violent impulses without stopping to think about the logical consequences of his actions. Although this is clearly Sinclair's attempt to dramatize the "beast in man" in naturalistic fashion, the reader is unprepared for this suddenly violent and irrational aspect of Jurgis's character. Indeed, Jurgis, whom Sinclair describes as a big, strong man, appears as meek as a lamb, responding to every new problem with "I will work harder"—until he discovers that Connor has blackmailed Ona into his bed and yields to blind rage and violence:

> To Jurgis this man's whole presence reeked of the crime he
> had committed; the touch of his body was madness to him—it set
> every nerve atremble, it aroused all the demons in his soul. It had
> worked its will upon Ona, this great beast—and now he had it,
> he had it! It was his turn now! Things swam blood before him,

and he screamed aloud in his fury, lifting his victim and smashing his head upon the floor. . . . In a flash he had bent down and sunk his teeth into the man's cheek; and when they tore him away he was dripping with blood, and little ribbons of skin were hanging in his mouth.

What takes the reader aback here is not the animal nature of the reaction, which is magnificently rendered, but its unexpectedness, as Sinclair has cautiously avoided mentioning Jurgis's physical nature up to now and avoids it again until his second attack on Connor.

Sinclair had never come to terms with the animal nature of man in his own life and avoided dramatizing it in his fiction except when absolutely necessary for plot development. There is no satisfying brawling or physical release of tension in *The Jungle*. There is little fun, dancing, or loving except during the wedding feast. There is no ecstasy of being, no passionate love or will to live, no sensual pleasure—only a desperate and dumb endurance arising from dulled senses. An aura of puritanism also pervades the book, manifest in the exaggerated reaction of Ona when she confesses Connor's sexual blackmail and in the short scene when Jurgis has a sexual encounter after Ona's death: "he went upstairs into a room with her, and the wild beast rose up within him and screamed as it has screamed in the jungle from the dawn of time." There are definite overtones of Jack London here, but it is anomalous to find London's atavistic language in the context of a commonplace sexual act. Although he had known and chosen want, Sinclair never really belonged to the world of the poor and the manual workers, and watched it from the outside with horror. London, who had lived in that world during his youth and known most of its facets, could give a more balanced and intimate picture of it, which did not exclude the simple joys of life.

After the remarkable unity of the first section of *The Jungle*, with its climax in little Antanas's death, and the emotional intensity of the relentless suffering of Jurgis and his family, which transcends the relative weakness of the characterization and leaves one emotionally drained, the reader is almost relieved to be able to dissociate his sympathies from Jurgis in the remainder of the novel, where Sinclair tries to make him into a thinker. After the death of his wife and son, and having abandoned the rest of the family to probable starvation, Jurgis is offered a hand by a farmer who needs help in the fields, including a decent salary and board with plentiful food—all of which should be welcome to a man in his situation. Instead, Jurgis turns the offer down contemptuously because the work will not last past November, never considering that he would be better off facing the winter in good physical shape and with over two hundred dollars saved than with nothing at all, or the pitiful fifteen dollars he manages to save before going back to Chicago after a spring and summer of tramping and occasional work. From a disciplined work-beast, Jurgis turns overnight into a pseudosocial critic, and Sinclair's approving commentary—"Jurgis was beginning to think for himself nowadays"—leaves the reader baffled. From that moment on, Jurgis becomes a puppet in his creator's hands—a puppet in whose fate the reader quickly loses interest, because he is no longer convincing.

Sinclair was aware that the ending of the novel was weak and blamed it on lack of money: "never have I been able to write a single thing as I would have liked to write it, because of money. Either I was dead broke and had to rush it; . . . Think of my having to ruin *The Jungle* with an ending so pitifully inadequate, because we were actually without money for food." This rationalization of the second and third sections of the novel is disingenuous, for it is preaching that weakens the ending, as well as the attempt to put Jurgis through a long series of jobs that comprise a Cook's tour of the manual workers' world, the political world, and the underworld. Worse, when Jurgis becomes a socialist, everything starts going well for him and he finds a compassionate and understanding employer. Had Sinclair ended *The Jungle* with chapter 21 and the climax of little Antanas's death, the novel, as an allegory of victimization, would have had a unity of theme and effect infinitely more powerful, without alienating the reader by belaboring themes already dramatized or by presenting socialism as a universal and miraculous panacea. Lack of money did not force Sinclair to ruin the ending of *The Jungle*; what did were his inability to leave well-enough alone and trust his readers to draw their own conclusions from the material presented, as well as his compulsive need to preach.

The natural and the urban jungles dramatized in these two novels have much in common. Both attest to the utmost survival skills, endurance, and the ability to overcome; and both are unforgiving of errors and unsparing of the weak. However, in the magnificent human allegory *The Call of the Wild*, natural instincts and animal nature are in harmony with the background, whereas in *The Jungle* they are self-destructive when pitted against the powerful industrial machinery of the stockyards. But the difference resides less in the indulging of instinctual urges than in the intelligent/unintelligent, imaginative/unimaginative, use of those instincts. Buck knows better than to pick a fight with Spitz before he can win it and uses all the forces he can master to weaken his enemy, exhibiting the infinite and elemental patience of the wild when survival is at stake. Jurgis, on the other hand, shows neither imagination nor patience in adapting to the world of the stockyards and, later, in taking vengeance on Connor. As a result, he remains an underdog despite his physical strength and hard work, and punishes himself and those he loves rather than Connor, who escapes with a few superficial wounds. Half equipped, Jurgis is lost between the animal and human worlds, never recognizing that to survive in a modern urban jungle one needs to exercise the same skills that enabled primitive man to survive. Buck is a hero with whom the reader can identify with exhilaration; Jurgis is a victim of his character and milieu whom the reader fears to recognize in himself, and therefore pities.

The major difference between these two jungles, however, is the presence or absence of beauty. However cruel, the natural jungle is beautiful and logical, while the man-made jungle is revolting and illogical. In the North, everything is gloriously pure and frozen. The beauty of the landscape and of Buck are breathtakingly rendered by London's lyrical prose. His depiction of an instinctual behavior perfectly suited to the environment, of emotionally satisfying immanent justice, of a joy in life shared by the most simple and complex organisms, and of a simple and primal relationship between life and death all testify that, with a few qualifications, London accepted the animal basis of human existence, and even reveled in it. In contrast, the setting of the human jungle is repulsive. Work in the stockyards is brutal; animal instincts are misused or missing, thus bringing about destruction; love of life and beauty are absent; and human feelings are deadened by drudgery and suffering. The social jungle is also irrational in its advocacy of virtues that bring about destruction and its condemnation of vices, such as corruption and prostitution, which allow for survival. Sinclair, unlike London, rejected man's animal nature and therefore only dimly perceived that survival, in both a complex human jungle and an amoral animal one, requires finely tuned animal instincts. But both the white and frozen northern wilderness with its redeeming purity and the urban world of pain, misery, and dumb endurance continue to exert a strong fascination as metaphors of man's animal past and present.

SCOTT DERRICK

What a Beating Feels Like:
Authorship, Dissolution, and Masculinity in
Sinclair's The Jungle

American naturalism owes much of its contemporary power to the success of its efforts to depict a thoroughly decentered subject. The naturalist text typically represents the determining impact of various and sundry social and natural forces on its characters and diminishes the importance of consciousness as the cause of the actions it records. Naturalist style, long criticized for lacking high modernist polish, actually contributes through its rawness to this effect. Rather than presenting themselves as intricate products of careful craftsmen, naturalist fictions such as *Sister Carrie* or *The Sea-Wolf* often seem hammered directly into being by a remorseless reality. Such novels ask for interpretation in terms of the broad social, political, and historical contexts favored by contemporary critical practices.

In addition to such broader contexts, however, attention to the figure of the author and to the structure of authoring are crucial to an understanding of the operation of gender in Upton Sinclair's *The Jungle*, which contains an unconscious narrative of Sinclair's self-creation as an author. This narrative does not obviate the social, historical, and political content of the text, but it suggests that a complex set of literary dynamics mediates the relation of text and world. These dynamics must be articulated with respect to the specific historical position of the author.

From *Studies in American Fiction* 23, no. 1 (Spring 1995). © 1995 by Northeastern University.

The Jungle is strikingly faithful to some of the most powerful contemporary critical accounts of naturalism, particularly in terms of naturalism's well-known relationship to Darwinian evolutionary thought and its complex genderings. Numerous commentators have argued that Darwinism substantially disrupted inherited patriarchal narratives of the structure of creation. As Christine van Boheemen concisely puts it, Darwin raises the possibility of "a suddenly powerful and prolific Mother Nature dethroning the ancient figure of God the Father." *The Origin of Species* in many ways conducts an effective dispersal of masculine authority, not only in its stunningly successful promotion of Mother Nature as the engineer of life's forms, but in its own manifold indeterminacies, its imaginative waywardness, its willingness to record and consider even conflicting positions within its own textual borders. In passing into cultural currency, however, Darwinism lent its authority to other constructions of gender, creativity, and selfhood. A potentially feminine "Darwinism"—using Darwin's proper name as a synecdoche for a host of cultural forces that Darwin's work both responded to and altered—generated a host of masculine authorities, among them canonical male naturalist authors like Sinclair, who countered its dispersals with synthesis, who found in its whimsicality and play iron social doctrines which supported aggressive, competitive masculine behaviors.

In Sinclair's *The Jungle*, "nature" seems characterized by the threatening fecundity one finds in Darwin's vision. Nature in Packingtown is characterized by an anxiety-inducing profusion of life, especially of children. In the first paragraph of the novel, for example, as Marija argues with a carriage driver in two languages, she is pursued by a "swarm of urchins." At the wedding of Jurgis and Ona, Sinclair tells us that the number of babies in attendance was "equal to . . . all guests invited." In a "collection of cribs and carriages . . . babies slept, three or four together." Later, Sinclair indicates that even the city dump, a place with "an odor for which there are no polite words," is "sprinkled over with children." Odors form a part of this profusion, as do the animals. One can smell Packingtown from miles away, with its "elemental odor, raw and crude; it was rich, almost rancid, sensual, and strong. There were some who drank it in as if it were an intoxicant; there were others who put their handkerchiefs to their faces." The ubiquity of odor is mirrored by the vast number of cattle, described in a way that suggests the vastness and heterogeneity of humanity itself: "as far as the eye can reach there stretches a sea of pens . . .—so many cattle no one had ever dreamed existed in the world. Red cattle, black, white, and yellow cattle. . . . The sound of them here was as of all the barnyards of the universe." The profusion of animals gives rise to a chaos of animal sounds: "The uproar was appalling; . . . one feared there was too much sound for the room to hold. . . . There were high squeals and low squeals, grunts and wails of agony."

The narrative's implicit fear of a world swarming with disreputable life and the sense of being entrapped by it eventually coalesces into a fear of family life, and, within the confines of the family, misogynistic fears of women and their reproductive powers. Capitalism is to blame for much of the suffering in the novel, yet as the title of the novel implies, Sinclair regards capitalism precisely as an unrisen nature into which humankind can periodically fall, or from which it can be transformed by the application of socialist principles. To the extent that Packingtown has its own "natural-ness" associated with physical terrors, its world is metonymically linked to women and their bodies.

Such a link is most evident at the single most wrenching scene in the novel, the death of Ona in childbirth. As the midwife, Madame Haupt, descends from the garret where Ona is dying, we are told that "she had her jacket off, like one of the workers on the killing-beds. Her hands and arms were smeared with blood, and blood was splashed upon her clothing and her face." Though this death is horrific, it also uncovers for Jurgis a previously veiled portion of reality, the hidden, horrible nature of nature. Sinclair tells us that "it was all new to him, raw and horrible—it had fallen upon him like a lightning stroke. When little Antanas was born he had been at work, and had known nothing about it until it was over; and now he was not to be controlled."

Eventually, *The Jungle* records not just a hatred of social injustice, poverty, and suffering, but an aversion to the body and all of its fluids, smells, and processes. Insofar as the novel reproduces the traditional equation between women and the body, this hatred is finally gynephobic. Prior to childbirth, the frail yet desirable Ona barely has a corporeal presence in the novel. Even at her death, *The Jungle* displaces its distaste for the female body and its biological processes onto the massive, fleshy figure of Madame Haupt. When Jurgis seeks the midwife, he finds her engaged in the affairs of the flesh, "frying pork and onions"; she seems to be the only immigrant in Packingtown who has enough to eat. Sinclair tells us that "she was a Dutch woman, enormously fat," and that "she wore a filthy blue wrapper, and her teeth were black." After rubbing her hands with a saucer of "goose-grease" in her kitchen—good luck, Sinclair explains—Madame Haupt goes to minister to Ona. When she emerges, the blood displayed on her person, signifying the horror of childbirth and of the natural, allows Ona to be rescued from the body once more, for one last sentimental scene; when Jurgis finally sees Ona, "she was so shrunken he would scarcely have known her—she was all but a skeleton, and as white as a piece of chalk."

A passage in the original version of *The Jungle*, published in *The Appeal to Reason* but edited out of the Doubleday edition, expresses the link between women's bodies and the stockyards themselves. "Cannot anyone in his right senses," Sinclair's narrator cries, "see that such troubles as Ona's must continue to be the rule so long as women, whom God in his infinite wisdom has condemned to be manufacturing machines, will insist upon having children just as if they were ordinary human creatures?" The narrator's irony indicates that women have unnaturally been made to labor in the industrial world, in contrast to the natural process of childbirth. But one of *The Jungle*'s anxieties, which here seems to be unconsciously expressed, is that the two are actually the same and that even childbirth, even women, are part of a nature in which reproduction is blind, mechanical repetition.

These repeated crossings of boundaries, between male and female, nature and culture, the workplace and the home, reflect the fundamental incoherence of naturalism itself. As *The Jungle* descends into its own jungle, the disjunctions and contradictions of naturalist metaphysics translate themselves into a fundamental crisis of selfhood as well, and this latter crisis is reflected in images of bodily disintegration, in the repeated dismembering and figurative castrations which the narrative records: the loss of fingers; the loss of feet; the loss of ears broken off in the cold; and, most horrible of all, the loss of little Stanislovas to rats. Shut in a dark cellar, he is cornered and eaten.

These fears of bodily disintegration are coterminous in the novel with fears of entrapment, as if a failure to rise from the body equals a life of imprisonment in an enveloping maternal womb that fundamentally undoes the illusion of autonomous masculine selfhood. As the novel progresses, it is increasingly dominated by images of enclosure in small dark spaces: in cellars and stairwells, prison cells, and basement workrooms, pits and abysses. These fears, in turn, produce or are produced by a claustrophobic masculine inability to tolerate the emotions of women. After Ona's rape by Connor, her anguish is so intense that Jurgis can "bear it no longer," and he "sprang at her . . . shouting into her ear: 'Stop it, I say! Stop it!'" Jurgis has a similar reaction to her tears during her pregnancy: "She had never been like this before . . . it was monstrous and unthinkable . . . the world . . . ought to kill them at once. . . . They ought not to marry, to have children . . .—if he, Jurgis, had known what a women was like, he would have had his eyes torn out first."

The need to escape the home becomes so overwhelming that Jurgis's unconscious desires uncannily produce the events of the narrative over which, in realist terms, he has no control. A series of scenes in this portion of the novel attests to the strength of Jurgis's desire to free himself from all family entanglements and to gain the masculine freedom of rural life. For example, after Jurgis's imprisonment for his attack on Connor, Ona's rapist, he simply concludes that death would serve his wife best: "the shame of it all would kill her . . . and it was best that she should die." Jurgis's wish for her death serves as a death sentence, and Ona soon perishes. Immediately after Jurgis is released from prison, he makes a mistake of astounding proportions. Even as he declares his willingness to "do battle" for his family against the world, he heads in the wrong direction on the strength of some bad navigational advice he receives from a child. After miles of journeying westward, a farmer informs him of his mistake. Jurgis quickly alters his course, but his legs have betrayed the direction in which he wants the developing narrative to carry him.

Ona's death and his devotion to young Antanas, his Nietzschean superbaby son, temporarily retain him in Chicago, but the narrative places Jurgis in an International Harvester factory, which once again sounds a proleptic note of rural life. And when the Harvester factory closes, he gains employment in a steel mill and uncannily encounters still another foreshadowing of his approaching flight. In one of the novel's most remarkable passages, Jurgis sees the protean molten steel as a kind of life essence, which assumes first a masculine shape, and then a determined and determining objective form. As he watches, the molten steel is a "pillar of white flame, dazzling as the sun . . . with a whiteness not of earth, scorching the eyeballs." In another place, where the "crashing" and "groaning" of machines seem like "the centre of earth, where the machinery of time was revolving," this cosmic plasma of molten steel becomes a phallic "great red snake escaped from purgatory" which "writhed and squirmed . . . until it was cold and black—and then it needed only to be cut and straightened to be ready for a railroad." At this point in the novel, what was formerly protean about Jurgis is similarly "cut and straightened" and unalterable. Several pages later, he will hop a passing freight train and ride these iron rails into the novel's curious rural idyll.

First, however, young Antanas, the last obstacle to the desire of the text, must perish in a death that itself serves as an uncanny foreshadowing of his father's flight. While Jurgis labors in the steel mill, Antanas bursts from a restricting house, plunges into a mudpuddle, and drowns. As a sobbing Marija informs Jurgis, "we just couldn't make him stay in." As a consequence, Jurgis makes his own break for freedom from a familial womb and is soon "peering out with hungry eyes, getting glimpses of meadows and woods and rivers." Once in the country Jurgis repeats Antanas's watery plunge, not in a puddle, but in a "deep pool, sheltered and silent," where he "splashed about like a very boy in his glee."

The uncanniness of this progress in the context of the rest of the novel is hardly liberating. On the contrary, this pattern of repetition contributes to the decentering of Jurgis's selfhood, as if the force which moves him were not recognizable as his own. Indeed, the novel is suffused with a horror of blind, mechanical repetition from beginning to end, which includes, but runs substantially deeper than, a hatred of the cycles of capitalism. In his rises and falls, Jurgis is encased in these mechanical repetitions, the most startling being the second attack on Ona's rapist, Connor, which reenacts the first: "precisely as before, Jurgis came away with a piece of his enemy's flesh between his teeth; and, as before, he went on fighting with those who had interfered with him."

These anarchic forces, however, are called to order through the intervention of Schliemann, the German intellectual whose authoritative socialist monologues offer explanations of the ills of the novel and propose regulatory solutions:

> Nicholas Schliemann was familiar with all the universe, and with man as a small part of it. He understood human institutions, and blew them about like soap-bubbles. It was surprising that so much destructiveness could be contained in one human mind. Was it government? The purpose of government was the guarding of property-rights, the perpetuation of ancient force and modern fraud. Or was it marriage? Marriage and prostitution were two sides of one shield, the predatory man's exploitation of the sex-pleasure. The difference between them was a difference of class. If a woman had money she might dictate her own terms.

Schliemann stands for a voice of absolute male intellectual authority, one that controls the body and its desires. According to Sinclair, Schliemann "studied the compositions of food-stuffs, and knew exactly how many proteins and carbohydrates his body needed. . . .That was the nearest approach to independence a man could make 'under capitalism,' he explained; he would never marry, for no sane man would allow himself to fall in love until after the revolution." At the same time, Schliemann has an erotic power over women, produced, evidently, by his intellectual greatness. As Jurgis listens to this disavowal of marriage, he notices a "beautiful young girl" listening to Schliemann "with something of the same look that he himself had worn, the time when he had first discovered Socialism." This "young college student . . . only spoke once or twice while Jurgis was there—the rest of the time she sat by the table in the centre of the room, resting her chin in her hands and drinking in the conversation."

The construction of such authority has been an important goal of the narrative all along, and once it is established, however ambivalently, Jurgis can be pushed to the margins like a spent puppet. Part of the unconsciousness which has been driving the novel, in other words, and part of what decenters Jurgis, is finally Sinclair's own will-to-authorship, which twines itself around the "proper" subject of the novel. The capacity magically to transform reality into the shape of desire is the prerogative of the author, the prerogative of the maker of narrative, and not a characteristic of actual experience as we know it.

The deepest desire of a writer often is to attain the position of author, a desire that often precedes—and hence underwrites—even the acquisition of a specific subject, which often results from a long and difficult search. Sinclair had an enormous desire for literary success early in his career and faced enormous difficulties in its pursuit. The roots of his desire to write, according to Sinclair's *Autobiography*, were located in a vision of the essential salubrity of genius he had had in the midst of his adolescence. In this vision, he imagines a kind of teetotaling boy's camp of literature, in which he could join a mix of great characters and great authors gathered around the fire:

> There was a campfire by a mountain road, to which came travelers who hailed one another and made high revelry there without alcohol. Yes, even Falstaff and Prince Hal were purified. . . . There came the melancholy Prince of Denmark, and Don Quixote. . . . Also Shelley. . . . I was laughing, singing, with the delight of their company.

Unfortunately for Sinclair, at the time of *The Jungle*'s composition, this vision of the felicity of literary success had not been realized in the realm of experience despite several efforts to produce literature of a monumental kind. One of these texts, *The Journal of Arthur Stirling*, took for its subject the fate of the man of "genius" trapped in a culture that fails to recognize and reward—and hence actively thwarts—his ambitions and abilities.

If Sinclair's ambition would make *The Jungle* a desperate project in any case, this desperation was augmented by the poverty in which he found himself at the time of his novel's composition and by the disintegration of his marriage. Sinclair wrote much of *The Jungle* in a small cabin he built himself in Princeton, New Jersey, as a space in which he could isolate himself from the problems of family life. His son David had been diagnosed with malnutrition and rickets in 1903, and his marriage to his first wife, Meta, had fallen into disrepair. Apparently acting out of a fear of fathering any more children who might complicate his life, Sinclair had adopted a regimen of sexual abstinence, arguing the common position of numerous health authorities that sexual activity ought to occur only for purposes of reproduction. One night, according to Leon Harris, Sinclair found his wife, Meta, in bed with a pistol, weeping because she was unable to pull the trigger. Sinclair himself readily admitted the connection between such unmitigated personal suffering and *The Jungle*:

> Externally, the story had to do with a family of stockyard workers, but internally it was the story of my own family. Did I wish to know how the poor suffered in wintertime in Chicago? I had only to recall the previous winter in the cabin when we had had only cotton blankets, and had put rugs on top of us and cowered shivering in our separate beds. It was the same with hunger, with illness, with fear. Ona was Corydon, speaking Lithuanian but otherwise unchanged. Our little boy was down with pneumonia that winter, and nearly died, and the grief of that went into the book.

Sinclair responded to such difficulties by increasing his commitment to writing, in pursuit of the kind of authorial success that promised rescue.

Because "author" is our culture's best metaphor for achieved humanist selfhood and the mastery of experience such selfhood implies, the story of becoming an author and the story of the genesis of selfhood are often intertwined and difficult to distinguish. Both will be highly inflected by gender in a culture in which subjects and authors are produced by the normative structures of nuclear family life. As the enterprise of psychoanalysis has made clear, a central task of the subject in the Western family is the management of gender difference and the consolidation of an identity as a heterosexual male or female. As a consequence, the materials an American author must manage in the course of becoming an author, the materials a subject must manage in order to compose identity, will always have a primary relation to gender.

A nineteenth-century male American author must have wrestled with gender in two respects. On the one hand, most men were raised by women and so necessarily receive much of their early training from feminine hands. At the same time, women are much more than mothers in American literature. As the imagined primary readers for the novel, as the active bearers and producers of cultural values, beliefs, and traditions, of poems, plays, and novels, women are real and substantial presences in American literature; nineteenth-century literary men experienced the prominence of women as a material reality and reacted to it.

The power of women's presence in American culture, in fact, is evident in what may be *The Jungle*'s most important literary predecessor. Sinclair apparently was partly inspired by *Uncle Tom's Cabin*, which he refers to in

Manassas as "the most unquestionable piece of inspiration in American fiction." According to Sinclair, nowhere in the world "is there a book more packed and charged with the agony and heartbreak of *woman*" (Sinclair's italics). Jack London, of course, famously called *The Jungle* the "*Uncle Tom's Cabin* of wage slavery," and Sinclair directly betrays a competitive relation to Harriet Beecher Stowe in the text of the recently recovered first edition: "She had many things in her favor which cannot be counted on by him who would paint the life of the modern slave. . . . Who can make a romance out of the story of a man whose one life adventure is the scratching of a finger by an infected butcher knife?"

If Stowe was a literary foremother, biographically Sinclair's mother had a substantial influence on the formation of his character. He remembered, for example, his mother reading to him from early childhood, and he was abysmally ignorant in his early schooling in the (masculine) business of mathematics. As he says in his autobiography: "I knew everything but arithmetic. This branch of learning, so essential to a commercial civilization, had shared the fate of alcohol and tobacco, tea and coffee; my mother did not use it, so neither did I." At the same time, his interest in reading alienated him from his alcoholic, navy-obsessed father:

> "The social position of a naval officer is the highest in the world," pronounced my father. "He can go anywhere, absolutely anywhere." . . . And meantime the little son was reaching out into a strange world of books; reading things of which the father had never heard. "What are you reading?" he would ask, and the son would reply, none too generously, "A book." . . . The chasm between the two was widening, never to be closed in this world.

Although Sinclair's mother was a key figure in his childhood and adolescence and helped form both his commitment to reform and his interest in literature, the author broke with her completely in later life apparently over issues of his own authority. According to Leon Harris, Sinclair told his son David at the time of her death, "she was the best of mothers up to about the age (my age) of 16. Then I grew beyond her, & she wouldn't follow, or couldn't. If she'd let me alone, it could have been all right; but she still thought I was a child & stubbornly fought to direct my life & *mind*. So for 35 years I could not meet her without a controversy starting."

As Sinclair's autobiographical writings underline, a paradox of naturalism, in and out of *The Jungle*, is that it produces images of female power which then pose problems for male identity. For example, Sinclair's Marija Berczynskas, located outside any and all conventions of feminine gentility, is the most remarkable and powerfully conceived character in *The Jungle*. In his account of the wedding which opens the text, Sinclair tells us that "it was all Marija Berczynskas. Marija was one of those hungry souls who cling with desperation to the skirts of the retreating muse. . . . Whether it was by beer, or by shouting, or by music, or by motion, she meant that it should not go." Moreover, Sinclair thought of himself as a kind of feminist man, and *The Jungle* clearly contains an explicit critique of marriage as a form of prostitution. Quite early in the novel Jurgis tries to buy Ona from her parents for his father's two horses. As Schliemann proclaims at novel's end, "marriage and prostitution were two sides of one shield, the predatory man's exploitation of the sex-pleasure." Indeed, Sinclair dedicates his autobiographical account of his troubled first marriage, *Love's Pilgrimage*, which he refers to as "this woman's book," to "those who throughout the world are fighting for the emancipation of woman."

In general, then, *The Jungle* massively and misogynistically defends against a feminine power that it creates itself. A crucial question of the text concerns a paradox central not only to *The Jungle*, but to the work of London, Norris, Dreiser, and much of naturalism. Why, if *The Jungle* enacts a construction of masculine authority, does it have an interest in powerful women instead of powerful men? The answer must be that naturalist masculinity involves disabling contradictions and fundamentally does not work, as its persistent depictions of men in various stages of fragmentation—often, literally as bodies in pieces—graphically indicate. The nineteenth-century insistence on separate spheres, in which men were raised *by women* toward masculine difference and autonomy, rendered the consolidation of masculine identity impossible. Female responsibility for childrearing guaranteed that men will come to contain qualities acquired from maternal sources. At the same time, rigid definitions of gender difference made it difficult to define these qualities as other than feminine. Gender difference in culture thus became gender difference within the masculine psyche, pushing naturalist masculinity into breakdown and disintegration.

Sinclair's novel clearly works to expose the inadequacy of Jurgis's conventional masculinity, ridiculing the conceit of his pride in his own self-sufficiency and strength. This assurance apparently has masculine origins, given that the text credits Jurgis's upbringing to his father and never mentions his mother at all. The adult Jurgis "could not even imagine how it would feel to be beaten. 'That is well enough for men like you,' he would say, '*silpnas*, puny fellows—but my back is broad.'" *The Jungle* will teach Jurgis, distinctly not a writer himself, what a beating feels like, as Sinclair gropes toward new forms of male identity.

The unmaking of Jurgis's masculinity, the exposure of its weaknesses and contradictions, creates space for an exploration of an alternative, "feminine" subjectivity. The forces of unleashed femininity, however, surface in the novel chiefly as a terrifying negation, necessitating the construction of a new form of masculine authority lest the novel share in Jurgis's abjection. The problem of this authority is, at the same time, the problem of how to find an ending for the narrative after the dissolution of its middle, an ending necessary if Sinclair's own act of authorship is to have a successful conclusion. At stake in this ending, finally, is the novel's capacity to imagine something like a fundamental transformation of late nineteenth-century conventions of gender, a transformation that can still supply an aesthetically necessary sense of narrative closure.

I have argued that the cold and clinical Schliemann represents one kind of male authority at the end of Sinclair's narrative. In fact, *The Jungle* has multiple and contradictory endings that work to qualify Schliemann's authority and create space for Sinclair's ambivalence about it. Schliemann's appearance in the text is preceded by another figure of intellectual authority, a widely passionate speaker who first wins Jurgis to socialism. This man, like Schliemann, has the power to transfix not only Jurgis, but a young and beautiful woman. Jurgis initially finds her presence at the public lecture disturbing:

> He turned a little, carefully, so that he could see her better; then he began to watch her, fascinated. She had apparently forgotten all about him, and was looking toward the platform. A man was speaking there. . . . A feeling of alarm stole over him as he stared at her. It made his flesh creep. What was the matter with her, what could be going on, to affect any one like that? . . . There was a faint quivering of her nostrils; and now and then she would moisten her lips with feverish haste. Her bosom rose and fell as she breathed, and her excitement seemed to mount higher and higher . . . like a boat tossing upon ocean surges.

The woman's response mirrors the emotional state of the speaker, whose power on the stage seems produced by his own borderline disintegration:

> It was like coming suddenly upon some wild sight of nature,—a . . . ship tossed about upon a stormy sea. Jurgis had an unpleasant sensation, a sense of confusion, of disorder, of wild and meaningless uproar. The man was tall and gaunt, as haggard as his auditor himself; a thin black beard covered half of his face, and

one could see only two black hollows where the eyes were. He
was speaking rapidly, in great excitement; he used many
gestures—as he spoke he moved here and there upon the stage.

As Jurgis listens, he feels a surfacing of unmasterable forces that represent a
transformation of his earlier abjection into bliss:

There was an unfolding of vistas before him, a breaking of the
ground beneath him, an upheaving, a stirring, a trembling; he
felt himself suddenly a mere man no longer—there were powers
within him undreamed of, there were demon forces contending,
age-long wonders struggling to be born.

It is difficult not to view homoerotic forces as among the ones liberated here,
particularly since Jurgis's conversion leads him to work in a hotel run by a
benevolent socialist aptly named "Tommy Hinds." Sinclair speaks of this
relation in terms that combine desire and fragmentation: "he would have cut
off one hand for Tommy Hinds; and to keep Hinds's hotel a thing of beauty
was his joy in life."

The body-shattering danger of these first relations requires the introduction of Schliemann, who, as opposed to the figure on the platform,
quietly sits "without emotions; with the manner of a teacher setting forth
to a group of scholars an axiom in geometry." It is Schliemann, finally, who
represents the power of male intellectual authority in naturalism to hold
the disruptions of the body, sexuality, and gender in check precisely by the
generation of an abstract account of them. At the same time, the voice of
Schliemann has little in common with the impassioned prose Sinclair
produces, or with the prose of the woman Sinclair invokes as his literary
predecessor, Harriet Beecher Stowe. Devoid of emotion, Schliemann also
seems devoid of literature and so represents a style of masculine authority
that suppresses the masculine writer.

The two speakers, then, suggest a masculinity divided between its
masculine and feminine selves and also divided between eroticized and
noneroticized male relations. The difference in the two editions of the novel
have similar implications. In the earliest edition of the novel, Sinclair makes
even more explicit the feminine aspects of the first speaker:

He was a man of electric presence, with a face worn thin by
struggle and suffering. The fury of outraged manhood gleamed
in it—and the tears of suffering little children pleaded in his
voice. He was represented in the papers as a man of violence, but
he had the tenderness of a woman.

The prominence of the feminine in this figure of authority coexists with a vulnerability to the disruptive presence of actual women. The novel ends with the interrogation of the "Pitchfork Senator" by a woman in the audience who will not be put in her place. The Senator tries mockery, saying, "I can face any man, but, my God, I'm not used to arguing with women." According to Sinclair, "the laughter over this would have cleared the atmosphere in any meeting less determined; but when it ceased, the woman was still there. She kept shaking her finger at the speaker—she would have answers." One page later, Sinclair refers to this women as the Senator's "Nemesis," as she leaps to her feet and interrogates him again. The speaker's vulnerability to the woman and her wagging finger, in turn, signals a continuing vulnerability for Jurgis Rudkus. As opposed to Schliemann's "solutions" to Jurgis's problems, the first edition returns him once again to prison, and so refuses to rescue him from the irrational repetitions of its plot. It thus also answers ambiguously the question of whether, for men, an underlying femininity is tolerable.

Taken together, the endings of *The Jungle* suggest naturalism's discontent with the masculine authority that, because of the imperatives of culture and the dynamics of literature, it also strives to compose. Its investment in depictions of a powerful and omnipresent femininity, finally, contains a wish that its own repressive structures be shattered as well as a fear that such a wish might be granted. It powerfully depicts male disintegration, and it uses the energy of disintegration to generate new forms of confining masculine power. It veers wildly from the iron rails of probability, and it clings desperately to the structure of normative masculine plots. It wrestles manfully with the appalling inconsistencies and contradictions of late nineteenth-century gender roles, but finally cannot transcend them.

MATTHEW J. MORRIS

The Two Lives of Jurgis Rudkus

William Dean Howells once warned that realism, like romance, would
ultimately die as a truthful art form: "When realism becomes false to itself,
when it heaps up facts merely, and maps life instead of picturing it, realism
will perish too." He meant that realism must show some of the pattern of
life, instead of merely accumulating description. That is a reasonable
program, although Howells chose puzzling terms: one might just as easily
have aligned "picturing" with formless description, and "mapping" with a
realism that discloses the underlying structure of events. What does a map
do if not subordinate surface appearances to a schema of spatial relations?
But Howells was stressing precisely the schematic quality of a fiction
congested with details. Such a fiction, having failed to identify the true
source of formal coherence in art as in life, would still aspire to meaning,
but this meaning could only be arbitrary, like that which is conventionally
assigned to the configuration on a map. Curiously, Howells' division of the
possible methods of realism here anticipates the analogous distinction
signalled by the title of George Lukács's "Narrate or Describe?" For
Lukács, classic realism surpasses naturalism in that realist novels take on a
narrative form dictated by or expressive of historical necessity, while naturalist novels, choked with description, remain formless. The true realist
must "go beyond crass accident and elevate chance to the inevitable,"

From *American Literary Realism: 1870–1910* 29, no. 2 (Winter 1997). © 1997 by McFarland &
Company, Inc.

which means dramatizing that epochal conflict in light of which every facet of the man-made world assumes significance. If he cannot see that conflict, though he may have the best intentions to promote reform by describing, for example, slum life, the novelist inevitably assembles discrete data whose significance he can only will as symbolic.

Lukács could thus have adopted Howells' vocabulary and said that naturalists like Zola, for all their virtuosity in description, lack the pictorial sense, and thus can only map social relations. Of course, Howells actually liked Zola, and Lukács based his aesthetic judgments on a theory of reification alien to the American novelist. Their dismissals of formless fiction coincide only in part. But this coincidence brings into focus some of the assumptions about realism that have informed responses to Upton Sinclair's *The Jungle*, a novel noted for its vivid descriptions and the ultimate formlessness of its plot, one which often seemingly "heaps up facts" in just the way that Howells (and, for different reasons and in different terms, Lukács) deplores. Sinclair must have been aware of the doctrines promulgated by Howells, and would later assent to censures of his novel which are at least consonant with these doctrines, if not derived from them. Yet *The Jungle* does not merely violate the canons of Howellsian realism, for it never quite embraces them. Rather, it remains, on the one hand, trapped within an ideal of factual accuracy which seemingly ignores Howells' call for formal harmony, while showing signs, on the other hand, of a more significant divergence from the realist program, a reclamation of romance as the indispensable dialectical counterpart of realism. In view of these signs, we must assume that the eccentricities of *The Jungle* have a constructive purpose, until they are proved to reflect poor judgment alone. The charge of "mapping" is unlikely to furnish such proof, for Sinclair arguably sets out to restore "mapping" to its literal sense: he uses spatial layouts as figures for complex social relations. When he describes how factories process meat, his description also functions as a diagram of how the ruling class corrupts democratic institutions.

This treatment of space is closely related to Sinclair's strategy of embodying capital, labor, and other abstractions in individual characters—another hallmark of what Howells calls "romance." But these authorial choices need not render a work shapeless or schematic. Sinclair's use of maps and types opens, rather than closes, the question of whether he fashions a compelling plot, one which supports the argumentative burden he places upon it. As a socialist, Sinclair believed that the environment shapes human behavior, but also that human beings may reshape their destinies. Men may not make their history just as they please, yet they do make it. Sinclair's treatment of characters, their settings, and their actions follows from this concern with the making of human beings and, or more properly within, their surroundings. To formulate the problem of realism and romance in Sinclair most clearly, then, we begin with a closely related matter: the proper role of personal development in a leftist literature which, as such, is in some measure bound to emphasize the impersonal or supra-personal conditions of collective action.

The most common plot in American radical fiction in the first half of the twentieth century, and particularly during the Progressive Era, depicted the conversion of a middle-class ingenue into an activist. Writers hoped, by showing such conversions, to induce similar changes in their audiences; they were also, understandably, writing about what they knew best, the processes of political discovery that had shaped their own vocations. They generally motivated these conversions by having characters observe, and if possible experience, the contrasts between rich and poor. The reader, following a fictive proxy through a series of telling juxtapositions, thus confronts the evidence that American society, rotten with class differences, can be saved only by socialism.

Although this strategy—portrayal of conversion, motivated by pointed comparisons—seems natural, indeed inevitable, the contradictions of novels like *The Jungle* call it into question. Everybody agrees that the first half of the novel, which shows the suffering of the Rudkus family under a system they can neither resist nor understand, is more compelling than the second half, in which Jurgis Rudkus comes to see and comprehend the class system that has destroyed everyone he cared about, and to join the fight to change that system. The concrete political effect of the novel followed from public furor over the quality of canned meat, so nauseatingly rendered in the novel's early going, and not from the later, programmatic introduction to socialist thought. Apparently Sinclair would have written a better novel in every way if he had forgotten about conversions and their motives.

Critics of Sinclair have often suggested the greatest danger of the conversion plot: if radical action is to come from the proletariat, fictions about the conversions of bourgeois protagonists, aimed at the conversion of bourgeois readers, are at best irrelevant, if not elitist. To be sure, *The Jungle* is one of the few Sinclair novels about the conversion of a worker, but critics have shown that even this story bears many traces of the detachment of its author and readers from the working class it purports to help. Michael Folsom argues that the tediously discursive ending of the novel reflects the lingering influence of its author's genteel background, which, at the crucial moment, got the better of his realist and socialist pretensions, and induced him to render Jurgis' conversion as "a psychic event, not a social or economic one." This psychologization makes the newly-politicized Jurgis less threatening to the middle class reader, in that the socialism he will help bring, far from being worker-culture, will feel like an extension of "polite society"; Jurgis' silence during the novel's final theoretical exposition attests to Sinclair's continuing concern more for the "intelligentsia" than for "laboring people." Thus the "tacked on," preachy quality of the final chapters reflects not merely the author's impatience to point his moral, but also his deeper political ambivalence about this moral.

Folsom's article defines a widely-shared view of the formal effects of ideology on "America's first proletarian novel." Christopher Wilson, discussing Sinclair's achievement and limitations as functions of the economics of publishing in the Progressive Era, argues that Sinclair in *The Jungle* assumes the position of a "visitor," a middle-class spectator whose detachment from the working-class tragedy he observes impairs his creative sympathy. Likewise, June Howard points out that Sinclair "plays the role of the reader's guide and interpreter in an alien land" so that "the worlds of the observer and the participant remain polarized, joined only by the narrator's pity and good intentions." Finally, L.S. Dembo, while joining Walter Rideout in defending the plausibility of Jurgis' conversion, finds in the best of Sinclair's later novels the same faults of intrusive spectatorship and class-condescension that Folsom and others have found in *The Jungle*.

The genteel protagonists of Sinclair's later novels, and the detached observer implicit even in *The Jungle*, all embody a wish: the wish that one could see the operations of class society from top to bottom, and choose the moral and rational response dictated by the plain facts. Above all, Sinclair wishes that the often invisible workings of class could become visible, indeed incarnate, and thus remediable; to show class struggle in the direct encounter of a rich man with a poor man, or in their close juxtaposition, is to show its solution, even if the encounter depicted remains one of violent injustice. The literary conventions which bring millionaires and proletarians face-to-face in this way are commonly described as "romantic" or "allegorical." As we have remarked, these terms generally carry a note of derogation, at least since Howells, who expressly links them. Now, when critics disparage Sinclair's willful and hasty allegories, they at least implicitly endorse an opposite method, a patient technique proper to realism. The genuinely realistic narra-tive follows its protagonists thought the great struggles of their lives and beyond, to the last consequences of these struggles, the ultimate social causes of which permeate every lived detail of the text, instead being of compressed into one or two symbols. By this measure, the most meticulously realistic part of Sinclair's oeuvre is the first twenty-one chapters of *The Jungle*, up until the death of little Antanas. To that point, every misfortune of the Rudkus family follows organically from the conditions of immigrant life in

Packingtown. Their suffering, if exceptional, is not incredible; it unfolds gradually, amid other, comparable, cases, in small matters as well as great, and despite their stubborn struggle for happiness and dignity. June Howard has remarked that an "inexorable fatality seems to purse Jurgis and his family, so that *The Jungle* at times seems to be following the logic of the plot of decline." Sinclair might well have followed this trajectory to the bitter end by letting Jurgis die, Hurstwood-style, after descending each remaining rung of the social ladder. Instead, he gives Jurgis a second life, with adventures as a tramp, a prisoner, a strikebreaker, a robber, a machine politician, again a prisoner, and finally a convert to socialism. I would argue that this second life is really no more allegorical than the first; it merely shifts its scene and themes, in order to relate the first life to a broader political context and to Sinclair's own professional experience.

Jurgis' first life, closely tied to the lives of his family, centers alternately on his workplace and his home, the house the family struggles to pay off and finally loses. As long as this poising of the Rudkus household against the stockyards predominates, the Rudkuses' ethnicity counts for something in the narrative; they struggle not only to survive, but also to preserve a certain community. By the time his father, wife, and son have died, however, Jurgis has lost this community, and the significance of ethnicity and of the first spatial system succumbs along with it. In Jurgis' second life, the narrator tries to show the causes of the earlier suffering in the workings of a political machine subservient to the great industrial machine he has already described. In this investigation a new spatial system prevails, now divided among various places where organized crime and political corruption block, deflect, or poison the flow of goods and information necessary to the well being of society. This spatial coding of social forces, like the allegorical presentation of social types, makes explicit tendencies to romance which are implicit even in the first part of the novel. The two halves of Sinclair's plot thus reflect two aspects of a single problem. In turning to the first half of the plot, then, we also take up the mix of political, rhetorical, and aesthetic theories which Sinclair brings to his problem.

I. THE FIRST LIFE: DESCRIPTION AND THE MELTING POT

Sinclair's criticism affirms the veracity of his fiction, at the expense of its fictiveness. Thus in response to reviewers' often vehement disagreements about the accuracy of *The Jungle*, he announced his commitment to an ideal of unmediated description: "I intend 'The Jungle' to be an exact and faithful picture of conditions as they exist in Packingtown, Chicago. I mean it to be true, not merely in substance, but in detail, and in the smallest detail. It is as true as it should be if it were not a work of fiction at all, but a study by a sociologist." He reserves the right to "dramatize" and "interpret," but makes no further concession here to the impact of authorial perspective on observation, for he believes the science of socialism preserves him from distorting the world he would describe. Marx and his expositors famously vacillate between using "ideology" as a pejorative epithet applicable to bourgeois philosophy and political economy, and using it to denote a universal and constructive component of the reproduction of society; for Sinclair only the former sense exists. He expresses this rudimentary notion of ideology most clearly in an essay that antedates *The Jungle*, "Our Bourgeois Literature— The Reason and the Remedy."

Sinclair opens his article by defining "bourgeois." He believes civilization is approaching the close of a "long evolutionary process." For two hundred years, Europeans have been wresting "political sovereignty" away from the aristocracy; now "industrial sovereignty" must likewise be won for the entire populace, and it must be won worldwide. The class that won the first stage of this struggle and must lose the second is the bourgeoisie, and the currently ascendant literature is "simply the index and mirror" of this ruling class, with all its familiar vices. In later years, Sinclair's most disciplined muckraking would come in his "Dead Hand" series (1918–1927), tracts exposing the venality and hypocrisy of organized religion, journalism, education, and art; here he anticipates this project in a couple of sentences: "The bourgeois civilization is, in one word, an organized system of repression. In the physical world it has the police and the militia, the bludgeon, the bullet, and the jail; in the world of ideas it has the political platform, the school, the college, the press, the church—and literature." While this is hardly a nuanced view of the relationship between class interests and ostensibly disinterested public discourses, it sustained Sinclair for decades of work as a socialist writer. His task was to expose "repression" in its subtle forms as well as its overt ones, and so to contribute to the world's progress toward the utopia of reason.

At first glance, this program has little to say about the shaping function of the writerly imagination, just as it begs the question of how anyone can be sure of his or her own scientific impartiality. As Earl Norton Lockard points out in his dissertation on Sinclair, "technique" is "subordinate" here, serving "primarily to make the writing clear," and this subordination is consistent with a theory which assumes propaganda on behalf of the working class to be the true end of art. This theory could logically compel the writer to abandon fiction altogether, if another medium offered better results. Yet both *The Jungle* and Sinclair's early aesthetic statements do imply that fiction achieves its rhetorical ends in ways different from other kinds of writing, that novelists present their truths with uniquely literary conventions. "Our Bourgeois Literature" is a good example of the ambivalence with which Sinclair makes this implication. He initially denigrates the role of literacy conventions when he accuses writers constrained to please a middle-class public of turning "all history into a sugar-coated romance," while socialist writers hew to the bitter unliterary truth. But later in the essay he speaks of "the mighty revolution that is gathering its forces, far down in the underworld of the poor," showing his attachment to a figurative system in which unveiling and eruption would remedy the burial and damnation of the poor under the existing regime. Such a system is more consistent with romance than with realism, to say nothing of the unmediated exposure of reality. Here, then, Sinclair makes his first dialectical leap from a program of description which merely ignores Howells, to a renewal of romance which potentially answers him.

Of course the "underworld" had long since become a dead metaphor, the isolated use of which means nothing, but we will see that this metaphor is hardly isolated in *The Jungle*. There the gustatory analogue for the writer's procedure will hardly be sugar-coating—one thinks rather of an emetic medicine—but the emphasis on a demonic world veiled by innocent surface appearances is fully consistent with a kind of romance. A further nonfictional clue to this (high literary) imaginative system of disguises, burials, exposures, and eruptions comes in "Is 'The Jungle' True?," where Sinclair declares that "The Beef Trust is a thing which presents itself to my imagination as a huge castle, a fortress of knavery and fraud," adding that he had to "descend into the social pit" to write about it. The figure of proletarian life as subterranean, and capital as a fortress, is an admission that literary conventions, and indeed conventions which antedate and survive any discussion of realism, animate Sinclair's "exact and faithful picture."

Sinclair approaches a similar admission in *The Jungle* itself, and even at a moment when he intends to emphasize the opposite, simply factual, aspect of his work. In a passage from the original serialized version of the novel, which was cut in the Doubleday, Page edition, the narrator maintains that his task as the spokesman for wage slaves is harder than the task of his model, Harriet Beecher Stowe. Her novel on the life of chattel slaves was dramatic and picturesque because the cruelty of masters and the flight of the runaway slave have great inherent literary interest, but "the lash which drives" the proletarian—economic need—"cannot either be seen or heard." This complaint, consistent with Sinclair's belief in unmediated reporting, hardly does justice to Stowe's inventiveness, and its excision improves the novel. But in elaborating this point, Sinclair reveals a curious ambivalence, notably when he asks "Who can make a romance out of the story of a man whose one life adventure is the scratching of a finger by an infected butcher knife, with a pine box and pauper's grave as the denouement?" On the one hand, this question implies that Sinclair's subject matter is unromantic—he might have said "naturalistic." But the sentence also implies that Sinclair would be willing, like his precursor, to use "romance" for his propaganda— if it were available and effective. Indeed, he admits elsewhere that he tried in *The Jungle* "to put the content of Shelley into the form of Zola"—surely the ambition of a writer who had at least considered appropriating the form of Shelley as well. Further, Sinclair's rhetorical question indicates that the raw materials of his novel come from life already incipiently formed as "stories" with "denouements," and hence that the writer cannot present them without considering how they function as plots. Sinclair disavows such considerations when he pretends to practice direct description, but his fiction everywhere belies this pretense. When he describes people and places, he invariably shows how both are caught up in processes of change.

The most rich and sustained descriptions of *The Jungle* are those of the *veselija* or wedding feast of Jurgis and Ona, in Chapter One. Having attended such festivities during his seven weeks of research in Packing- town, Sinclair was able to show the customs of the Lithuanian immigrants in some detail. In doing so, he introduces the family and establishes its utter difference from the American mainstream. But this chapter already hints that the immigrants' customs have begun to erode in America. For instance, Jurgis and Ona trust their wedding guests to contribute cash to offset the expense of the entertainment, but these contributions fall short of the expected amount. The sense of communal obligation which would have motivated the guests in Lithuania has already begun to wither under "some subtle poison in the air" of the new country. The poison is the narrow understanding of self-interest, made ever narrower by the pressures of the free market. Thus the young couple starts its life together burdened with debts and baffled by social change; it is already engaged in the action which will transform it irrevocably. The same action continues through the second great descriptive set piece of the novel, the factory tours of Chapter Three. For the family members, not privy to the commentary in which Sinclair debunks the packers' propaganda, leave the tours too awe-struck to suspect the deceit and violence they will soon find in this workplace. As a result, before they begin consciously to struggle, they slide even further from knowing and resisting their antagonists. After these tours and the family's purchase of a house in the next chapter, all of the decisive environ- mental factors are established, and the human experiment begins to unfold more rapidly and inexorably. The contradictions of the ensuing narrative follow from Sinclair's effort to balance the ethnic difference of the

Rudkuses against the political imperative to make their metamorphosis typical for all American workers, and so to allegorize.

By the end of the novel, Sinclair ceases to pay attention to the specifically Lithuanian qualities of the Rudkus family. Their fate becomes nothing more or less than representatively proletarian. But it would not be fair to say that Sinclair's interest in their ethnic peculiarities was factitious, an opportunistic injection of color into the beginning of the story. Rather, Sinclair meant to show how industrial capitalism, among its other effects, could strip away the uniqueness of folkways as it transformed immigrant farmers into industrial workers. The house the Rudkuses buy, to their ultimate grief, is where this process of stripping-away emerges as representative. As their neighbor, Grandma Majauszkiene, relates in Chapter Six, four earlier families—German, Irish, Bohemian, and Polish—have successively bought and lost the same house. Her urban archeology is highly conscious of differences among these ethnic groups; she notes, for instance, that the Irish family used political clout to stave off its doom for a while. And yet these differences cannot measure up to the regularity with which the house, and by extension the economic world it represents, works the same fateful transformations on the families. Sinclair exaggerates when he implies, by the example of this house, that every new family was destroyed by Packingtown. In reality, each wave of immigrants found a place, however slowly and painfully, in American society. Thus James R. Barrett points out that the German and Irish workers who first came to the stockyards had become "the most 'American'" and the best adjusted by 1909, while the Bohemians were on their way toward Americanization. In this perspective, the outright annihilation of the Rudkus family is a figure for the cultural bleaching it would undergo if, like most families, it survived.

By using this house to concentrate the social forces that corrode ethnic identity, Sinclair reminds us that naturalism is often defined as a kind of fiction which uses heavy description to promote a genetically or environmentally deterministic theory. But even the crudest materialism understands the environment to encompass more than the local physical surroundings, and certainly Sinclair's socialism is refined enough to recognize that the Rudkus house is more suggestive as a symbol than as a direct source of unexpected bills, unsafe sidewalks, and unclean water. Bad as these conditions are, they are secondary to the house's status as the intended reward for the family's labors, and its haven from a hostile world. When the family loses the house, a series of non-homes (brothels, prisons, thieves' dens, streets) takes its place, until Jurgis finds a new, indestructible family in socialism, and a correspondingly collectivized home in the hotel of Comrade Tommy Hinds. The novel's scenes of degradation thus appear as stages in Jurgis' progress from traditional to revolutionary community, which means that the setting has an allegorical function, in the novel's vision of human renewal, from the first. It also means that this allegory, far from being the negation of purposeful plotting, always emerges through an action, a process of change.

Although the Rudkus house and neighborhood are important scenes of transformation in their own right, the greatest changes unfold when the narrative moves out into the workplace. What happens there, in turn, both influences public life and is affected by it. This interplay of economy and polity emerges as the explicit topic of the novel's later chapters, but it is already implicit in the first life of Jurgis Rudkus. As early as the ninth chapter, for example, Sinclair suggests that political disfranchisement is systematically united with the family's other woes. The chapter opens with a report on how venal Democratic Party operatives induce the immigrant workers to sell their votes, and then describes how the officials thus elected allow the packers to pollute the environment and adulterate meat. But this outline of systemic corruption must remain imperfect until reader and protagonist have both felt the full subjective horror of the results. Jurgis, in particular, must experience effects before he can understand causes. And so Sinclair goes on to catalogue the special debilities incidental to each job in the packinghouse: workers in the pickle rooms contract infections, and have their fingers eaten away by acids; butchers and can-makers cut their hands up, while stampers' hands simply get chopped off. Finally, in a painful literalization of the metaphor of the American city as cultural melting-pot, workers in the cooking rooms fall into huge cooking vats, perhaps only to be fished out after "all but the bones of them had gone out to the world as Durham's Pure Leaf Lard!" This most extreme variant of the immigrants' forcible assimilation exemplifies how all the descriptive passages in the first life of Jurgis Rudkus are indeed allegorical, even fabulous, but hardly formless. The injuries and adulterations they detail contribute to a larger narrative: of the destruction of a family, and the poisoning of a commonwealth. We cannot understand the completion of this narrative, the tale of redemption, merely by labelling it as a failure in Sinclair's skill and patience as a writer, his rigor as a socialist, or his purity as a realist. We may, though, be able to show how his vocational trials affected the kind of allegory he wrote as he moved his protagonist out of the stockyards.

II. THE SECOND LIFE: MAPPING THE JUNGLE

In the second life of Jurgis Rudkus, Sinclair offers a more complete systemic view and causal analysis of the evils of the modern industrial city.

This change of focus, from the experience of injury to the elucidation of causes and remedies, brings with it an increasingly deliberate reflection on the nature of political knowledge. Although Sinclair believes in the ultimate rationality of history, and hence in the worldly efficacy of writing exposés, he is wary of piecemeal political interventions, like the arrest of individual crooked aldermen and corporate malefactors. Such interventions constitute a reformist counter-narrative which steals and blunts the truths of the socialist movement, leaving the profound structural evils of capitalism intact. This co-optation may be the least brutal weapon of a ruling class which, as we have seen Sinclair saying in "Our Bourgeois Literature," still has its police, bullets, and bludgeons as well. But for Sinclair as a writer, the subtler intellectual weapons of the bourgeoisie pose a profoundly personal threat. I suggest that he became increasingly conscious of this threat as he turned to the second life of Jurgis Rudkus. This tale of proletarian education is thus also a report on historical and journalistic revisionism, and the predicament of the writer who would combat these evils. Sinclair's later chapters make most sense when seen in the light of this predicament. He is now writing about transformations of literary meaning, as well as economic and political life. Critics have had trouble seeing this widening of the novel's vision of change, because Sinclair himself, discussing the composition of the later parts of *The Jungle*, emphasized the loss of meaning, rather than its displacement. Reading the later chapters of the novel thus entails reconsidering Sinclair's discussion of what went wrong while he wrote it.

Sinclair believed that his "last chapters were not up to standard" because he had lost "both my health and my money" over the course of 1905. His account of how he wrote the novel does not specify when this decline set in, or which chapters first bear witness to it, but other sources lend some substance to his claim. Sinclair reports that he began writing on Christmas Day, 1904, and worked steadily for three months. By the end of this time (25 March 1905), four chapters of the serial had run in as many weekly issues of the socialist journal *The Appeal to Reason*, whose managing editor, Fred Warren, had the first nine chapters two weeks before running the first installment on February 25. Thus Sinclair composed at least half of the first life in six weeks, and several more chapters before taking his family on a spring vacation in Florida. Beginning in May with the tenth chapter, the weekly installments consist of half-chapters, until the death of Ona in Chapter Nineteen, which ran on August 26. This change may reflect a slackening of Sinclair's pace of production, a decline which would be consistent with more concrete evidence that he was becoming distracted or discouraged by late summer. Sinclair reports that he went to work founding the Intercollegiate Socialist Society "shortly before the completion of the book." Since the I.S.S. had its inaugural meeting on 12 September 1905, it seems likely that Sinclair finished the novel in late September or early October. By then he had ascertained that Macmillan would not grant the request he had made in a letter on September 13 for a second five hundred dollar advance with which to rework the later chapters as the sequel to a first novel consisting essentially of the first life. The last serial installment appeared in the *Appeal* on 4 November 1905, while the quarterly *One Hoss Philosophy* had carried a somewhat different conclusion to its concurrent run of the novel in October. The following January, Sinclair, having had further differences with Macmillian and four other publishers, signed a new contract with Doubleday, Page, which published the revised novel in February.

Thus by the end of the serial run, Sinclair, experiencing friction with both socialist and commercial editors, was looking for ways to reconceive his task. The conditions under which the very last chapters appeared imply that they were especially damaged by this stress, as their plodding quality would seem to suggest. Warren ran the last eight chapters (including the ones that consist almost exclusively of doctrinal exposition, and are equivalent to the last four chapters in the Doubleday, Page edition) in a separate package which readers had to request by postcard, a sign that popular interest in the serial had waned. It is even possible that Sinclair had seen some of the negative reader reports which were circulating at Macmillian, a factor which could have demoralized him as he wrote his didactic peroration. Yet the author's merely privative view of how the novel's second half differs from its first is insufficient. Even if such a view held for the very last, homiletic, chapters, it would remain inadequate for Chapters Twenty through Twenty-Seven, the bulk of the second life. Though we may never know enough about the quotidian details of the composition of *The Jungle*, I suggest that as Sinclair experienced personal reverses in the summer of 1905, he became increasingly conscious of parallels between himself and his protagonist. But even if these reverses came too late to affect the content of the second life, Sinclair's earlier travails as a writer had predisposed him to identify with industrial workers, and this predisposition is the key to his emerging emphasis on textual as well as industrial and cultural retooling.

Sinclair was the first to discuss this identification, presenting it as a source of strength which had benefitted *The Jungle*: "I wrote with tears and anguish, pouring into the pages all the pain which life had meant to me. Externally, the story had to do with a family of stockyard workers, but internally it was the story of my own family." He adds that Ona and her infant parallel his first wife Meta and their son David, both of whom were sickly, and he relates how the entire family, like the fictional immigrants, faced the budgetary constraints which come with an ambitious mortgage. So while it is always dangerous to equate writer and protagonist, the author here offers a warrant for seeing some such identification imparting vividness to the novel's early narrative of economic struggle. Leon Harris has pursued this connection into the second life, comparing Jurgis' stint as a migrant agricultural worker and tramp to Sinclair's attempt to write while living in the country. Of course, observing such parallels does not, in itself, address the problem of how Sinclair's narrative generates meaning after it abandons its first spatial system. The same writer who draws inspiration from a little bit of adversity could, after all, be ruined by a lot of it; such a view of Sinclair's case would be compatible with his autobiographical assertions, but it would bring us no closer to understanding what the later chapters actually do. To gain that understanding, and finally read the maps rather than simply dismiss them, we need to consider a topos in Sinclair's confessional writings which has a sustained and thematic relationship with the topography of his novel: the use of prison to symbolize ideological error.

Sinclair describes his conversion to socialism as "the falling down of prison walls about my mind." This sentence comes from an autobiography he wrote in 1932, but coincides with images which appear in his non-fiction at least as early as "Is 'The Jungle' True?," with its capitalist "fortress of knavery and fraud." Prison is a conventional, even trite, figure for illusion or ignorance, but for that very reason we may assume a certain constancy of meaning among Sinclair's uses of it. Such constancy, within a given text, is one of the distinguishing features of allegory; I am suggesting that references to prison in *The Jungle* have this allegorical consistency, but also that later works by Sinclair enable us to see these references as something more than the feverish effusions of a hurried and impoverished writer.

In *The Brass Check* (1920), his exposé of the kept press, Sinclair relates an episode which preceded, and may well have influenced, his work on *The Jungle*. In 1904 Sinclair, newly converted to socialism, wrote "An Open Letter to Lincoln Steffens," asking the author of *The Shame of the Cities* what practical remedies he proposed for the abuses he had documented. Steffens liked the letter and tried to get *McClure's* to publish it; refused, it found its way to *Collier's*, where the young editor Robbie Collier accepted it until his father, the publisher, compelled him to reverse the decision and keep the magazine free of subversive messages. Sinclair renders this reversal dramatically, as a personal affront he endured while dining with the Colliers. He then describes their refusal to publish his letter as a cause of the 1919 Red Scare: if *Collier's* had "taken up the truth which I put before them, they would have conducted a campaign to make the American people see it—and to-day we should not be trying to solve the social problem by putting the leaders of the people's protest into jail." Sinclair could hardly have sustained the grandiose historical claim which, taken literally, he makes here, but what matters is that he ties censorship to incarceration, and does so in connection with his vocational development. This development is a vital context for his great novel. In *The Jungle* as in *The Brass Check*, Sinclair uses the physical and ideological apparatuses of law to represent the forces that restrict radical literary expression, forces correlated in turn to the more subtle and constructive agencies that shape and distort public opinion. The series of confinements and escapes experienced by Jurgis Rudkus, however plausible in their own right, thus refer also to their author's struggle to convey through them the knowledge he had acquired about life in the stockyards, a struggle at once with a hostile publishing climate and a broader ideological environment resistant to the truths of socialism.

The episode with the Colliers in *The Brass Check* supports the view that this struggle was still on Sinclair's mind in 1920. It was presumably a fresher wound when he wrote *The Jungle*, where it enters into a scene from Chapter Twenty-Four, familiar to viewers of Charlie Chaplins' *City Lights*. The drunken son of one of the great meat-packing tycoons picks up Jurgis, takes him home, feeds him sumptuously, and gives him a hundred-dollar bill. After the young man passes out, the butler throws Jurgis back on the street; Jurgis is robbed of his hundred dollars by a bartender, whom he assaults, only to be arrested. The episode stresses human connectedness by the irony that the young man whose fortune depends on the daily exploitation of people like, and at times including, Jurgis, can casually and meaninglessly give him such a sum; it is in part a parody of private charity. It is also unapologetically allegorical, both because its characters are all types, and more narrowly because it presents Jurgis' arrest as the mere external realization of a spiritual shackling which antedates the encounter with the bartender: "all outdoors, all life, was to him one colossal prison, which he paced like a pent-up tiger, trying one bar after another." This sentence, so redolent of Sinclair's apprenticeship as a hack writer, anticipates Sinclair's introduction to the chapter of *The Brass Check* about his famous interview with President Theodore Roosevelt. In the middle of a series of chapters on the publication and reception of *The Jungle*, and its deflection from its real goals, Sinclair pauses to recall his resolution and the adversity that tested it: "I was determined to get something done about the Condemned Meat Industry. I was determined to get something done about the atrocious conditions under which men, women, and children were working in the Chicago stockyards. In my efforts to get something done I was like an animal in a cage. The bars of this cage were newspapers, which stood between me and the public; and inside the cage I roamed up and down, testing one bar after another, and finding them impossible to break." Sinclair's representation of the writer as a caged animal fits neatly with his

admission that he identified with his protagonist. The same metaphor applies
to Jurgis' unfreedom wherever he goes, and Sinclair's incapacity to help,
however he writes. Jurgis' adventures reflect his creator's career: as surely as
Jurgis is thrown out of the packer's mansion by the butler, Sinclair finds
himself turned out of the house of Collier.

Just as Sinclair figures himself as a struggling worker, Jurgis emerges
as a prototype of the proletarian writer. This emergence lends plausibility
to his conversion, as it shows him assembling a narrative picture of the
world he has experienced. He does so, appropriately, by moving between
the extreme immurement of the convict, and the total exposure of the
homeless beggar. First he becomes "free to roam the shopping district,"
observing its contrasts; this freedom comes after his first imprisonment,
but before the encounter with the millionaire, and the confinement that
follows it. His compensation for this enforced, and in many ways degrading,
sojourn in the wide world of contrasts is not merely an increase in street-
wisdom ultimately redeemable as socialist doctrine, but also, more proxi-
mately and specifically, the acquisition of the ability to narrate. When, after
further adventures, he becomes a successful beggar, he does so by
constructing a "hard-luck story," of which "not a word . . . was true," but
which he can deliver "scientifically." He has become a romancer, in short—
and one who, like a good naturalist, brings science to his narration. In the
penultimate chapter of the serial, Jurgis, now a socialist, even finds his voice
as an orator, joining his comrades in debate with a reactionary politician. By
making himself conspicuous in this way, he exposes himself to a final arrest
for an assault committed in his old life, but this time the walls and bars
around him will be purely physical. Meanwhile, by making his surrogate a
skilled purveyor of rogue stories, Sinclair virtually admits that his own development as a writer and a socialist, and his decision to turn Jurgis' life into a
picaresque tale, were positively shaped by his engagement with the great
resources of romance writing.

With this engagement in mind, we are better equipped to understand
the rhetorical strategy of the second life of Jurgis Rudkus. The novel
certainly shifts mode and mood between the first twenty-one painful chapters, in which the Rudkus family is ground into sausage, and the next six
chapters, in which Jurgis wanders about, mixing with rich and poor, and
learning the ways of tramping, corrupt city politics, and organized crime.
The man who can move among these different worlds is a definitive medi-
ator among types, and in playing this role Jurgis loses all personal specificity
(i.e., as a stockyards worker, as a Lithuanian). But the claim that this change
of narrative method represents a loss of realism is hard to sustain, or even
define; we have seen that the first half already contains a strong tendency to

romance. With the close of this half, the novel shifts its focus from the family's struggle to preserve a certain community to the causes and consequences of its failure in this struggle. In the second half Jurgis has no home, but the factory remains, now part of the series of equivalent infernos, jungles, and jails, each of which symbolizes the repression of writing and memory. In this world Jurgis the adventurer is as free of social bonds as Sinclair the observer, for whom he becomes a surrogate. Before, Sinclair contrasted industrial efficiency with personal and ecological chaos; now the scenes of blockage and pollution also refer, however obliquely, to a damming-up of information, a poisoning of public opinion.

This subtext of censorship and revision enters into almost all of the novel's later maps, however schematic they appear, and however far they depart from the setting of the early chapters. For example, one of the temporary jobs Jurgis finds after his family breaks up involves helping to build a freight subway, "a perfect spider-web beneath the city." Although the city council has only authorized "the construction of telephone conduits under the streets," a group of capitalists is using the contact to set up a freight monopoly; they intend "to have the teamsters' union by the throat." The episode thus contributes both to the novel's titular conceit (metropolis as wilderness, complete with throat-ripping predators) and to its allied project of using the city's geography and architecture to give physical substance to the intangible evils of capitalism. For this project, the unauthorized digging is more suggestive than the Yerkes traction scandals which Dreiser was to fictionalize in *The Titan*, though these latter were more notorious, and Sinclair does mention them, too. The street railways Yerkes sought to corner were mainly elevated, and thus less infernally resonant than the tunnels into which Jurgis descends. But Sinclair has a second reason for displacing affect from the traction scandals to the buried "spider-web." For this scheme does not merely menace labor, but also perverts the city council's well-meaning effort to facilitate communication. The contractors promise to enhance the flow of information by deploying telephone lines, and deliver instead a system for transporting freight, one which will ultimately, upon the death of the union and the consolidation of the monopoly, impede the free circulation of goods and ideas alike. Sinclair regularly links these two forms of circulation and the blockages which threaten them, and this linking complements his identification of the writer and the worker. Characteristically, he dismisses the official investigation of the telephone scheme by highlighting its literary character: the malefactors may get into "gaol," but only "figuratively speaking."

Prison and its equivalents are thus scenes of literary contention, scenes that the enemies of reform deny, rewrite, or at least misname.

Where Sinclair the socialist sees a jungle, bourgeois political economists see Nature; where he sees an inferno, they see an efficient machine; where he sees jail and silence, they see law and necessity, the triumph of fact. Each of these re-visions leads directly to the next. For example, when Jurgis is first incarcerated, Sinclair speaks of his jail as a "Noah's ark" of crime and a "wild beast tangle," equating prison with a jungle. Later, when Jurgis is a beggar, Sinclair calls the Detention Hospital into which beggars are herded "a miniature inferno," but also, in effect, a jungle, whose residents can be seen "barking like dogs [and] gibbering like apes." Hell, jail, and jungle are thus interchangeable terms, and all three are scenes of blockage, the squandering of human capital. But Sinclair's deepest insight is that mere waste is impossible: the capitalists have, rather, created vast laboratories, places of mutation, ideological as well as physical. They preside over something far more terrible, and far more wonderful, than any ordinary abattoir, just as Sinclair writes something far more complex than a botched naturalist novel.

A muckraker must show industrial conditions in their full hideousness, as the reality underlying the utopias of the political economists, and yet he must also show the efficiency of the system that exploits these conditions and extends them even to the writer's cell. In other words, his task of making the terrible transformative powers of capitalism visible is inseparable from his discovery that anything he says must take its place among existing representations—that his observation of reality is intertextually mediated. Sinclair never formed an adequate theory of the relationship between inherited literary form and realistic depiction, but the growing explicitness within his novel of the romantic animation of the landscape, and the change in Jurgis' representative function, attest to his struggle with this relationship. This struggle has been seen only in negative terms, as the reason the novel unravels. Now we can understand it as a positive adaptation of the novel's code.

Chronology

1878	Born on September 20 in Baltimore, Maryland, to Upton Beall and Priscilla.
1888	Family moves to New York City.
1892	Enrolls in College of the City of New York.
1897	Writes novels to finance education at Columbia University.
1900	Marries Meta H. Fuller.
1901	*Springtime* and *Harvest* is published. In December, son David is born.
1903	*The Journal of Arthur Stirling* is published.
1904	*Manassas* is published. Travels to Chicago to research for *The Jungle*.
1906	*The Jungle* is published. Founds Helicon Hall in Englewood, New Jersey, an experiment in communal living.
1907	*The Metropolis* is published.

1907   Helicon Hall destroyed by fire. *The Money-Changers* is published.

1911   *Love's Pilgrimage* is published.

1912   Divorces in Amsterdam.

1913   Marries Mary Craig Kimbrough in Virginia.

1915   Moves to California.

1917   *King Coal* is published. Resigns from Socialist Party but later rejoins.

1918   *The Profits of Religion* is published.

1919   *Jimmy Higgins* is published.

1920   *The Brass Check* and *100%* are published.

1923   *The Goose-Step* is published.

1924   *The Goslings* is published.

1925   *Mammonart* is published.

1927   *Oil!* is published.

1928   *Boston* is published.

1930   *Mental Radio* is published.

1932   *American Outpost* is published.

1933   *Upton Sinclair Presents William Fox* and *I, Governor of California* are published.

1934   Wins Democratic nomination for Governor of California; narrowly loses election.

1935   *I, Candidate for Governor* is published.

1936	*Co-Op* is published.
1937	*The Flivver King* is published.
1940	Begins Lanny Budd series with *World's End*.
1941	*Between Two Worlds* is published.
1942	*Dragon's Teeth* is published.
1943	*Dragon's Teeth* wins Pulitzer Prize. *Wide Is the Gate* is published.
1944	*Presidential Agent* is published.
1945	*Dragon Harvest* is published.
1946	*A World to Win* is published.
1947	*Presidential Mission* is published.
1948	*One Clear Call* is published.
1949	*O Shepherd, Speak!* is published.
1953	*The Return of Lanny Budd* is published.
1956	*The Cup of Fury* is published.
1960	*My Lifetime in Letters* is published.
1961	Mary Craig Sinclair dies at age 78.
1962	Marries May Hard. *The Autobiography of Upton Sinclair* is published.
1967	May Hard Sinclair dies on December 18.
1968	Dies on November 25 in New Jersey.

Note: The list of works above includes Sinclair's major works but is not exhaustive.

Contributors

HAROLD BLOOM is Sterling Professor of the Humanities at Yale University and Henry W. and Albert A. Berg Professor of English at the New York University Graduate School. He is the author of over 20 books, including *Shelley's Mythmaking* (1959), *The Visionary Company* (1961), *Blake's Apocalypse* (1963), *Yeats* (1970), *A Map of Misreading* (1975), *Kabbalah and Criticism* (1975), *Agon: Toward a Theory of Revisionism* (1982), *The American Religion* (1992), *The Western Canon* (1994), and *Omens of Millennium: The Gnosis of Angels, Dreams, and Resurrection* (1996). *The Anxiety of Influence* (1973) sets forth Professor Bloom's provocative theory of the literary relationships between the great writers and their predecessors. His most recent books include *Shakespeare: The Invention of the Human*, a 1998 National Book Award finalist, and *How to Read and Why*, which was published in 2000. In 1999, Professor Bloom received the prestigious American Academy of Arts and Letters Gold Medal for Criticism.

TIMOTHY COOK has been a senior lecturer in the School of Arts and Languages, Kingston Polytechnic, England. He has had essays published in *The Kipling Journal* and *Notes and Queries*.

SCOTT DERRICK is Professor of English at Rice University. He is the author of *Monumental Anxieties: Homoerotic Desire & Feminine Influence in 19th-Century U. S. Literature*.

MORRIS DICKSTEIN is a professor at Queens College, the City University of New York. He is the author of *Keats & His Poetry: A Study in Development* and *The Revival of Pragmatism: New Essays on Social Thought, Law, & Culture*.

EMORY ELLIOTT is a professor of English at the University of California, Riverside. He is the author of *Puritan Influences in American Literature* and the editor of a number of titles, including *The Columbia History of the American Novel*.

MICHAEL BREWSTER FOLSOM was a research associate in American Studies at the Massachusetts Institute of Technology, where he was Director of the New England Mill Studies Project. He was the editor of *Mike Gold: A Literary Anthology* and co-editor of *The Philosophy of Manufactures*.

RABINDRA N. MOOKERJEE was Professor of English and Dean of Graduate Studies at Sukhadia University, Udaipur, India, until his retirement in 1993. He is the author of *Art for Social Justice: The Major Novels of Upton Sinclair*, as well as a book on Theodore Dreiser.

MATTHEW J. MORRIS has been a visiting assistant professor at the College of Charleston.

JACQUELINE TAVERNIER-COURBIN is Professor of English at the University of Ottawa. She is the author of *Call of the Wild: A Naturalistic Romance*, as well as *Ernest Hemingway's "A Moveable Feast": The Making of Myth*.

JON A. YODER previously directed the American Studies program at Idaho State University. He published works in *American Studies* and *Rendezvous*.

Bibliography

Barrett, James R. *Work and Community in the Jungle: Chicago's Packinghouse Workers, 1894–1922.* Urbana and Chicago: University of Illinois Press, 1987.

Becker, George J. "Upton Sinclair: Quixote in a Flivver." *College English* 21 (December 1959): pp. 133–40.

Benson, Peter. "Possession and Dispossession in Crevecoeur's, Sinclair's, and Dos Passos's America." *Bridges: An African Journal of English Studies* 4 (December 1992): pp. 91–112.

Blinderman, Abraham, ed. *Critics on Upton Sinclair.* Coral Gables: University of Miami Press, 1975.

Bloodworth, William A., Jr. *Upton Sinclair.* Boston: Twayne Publishers, 1977.

Buitenhuis, Peter. "Upton Sinclair and the Socialist Response to World War I." *Canadian Review of Americn Studies* 14, no. 2 (1983): pp. 121–30.

Cantwell, Robert. "Upton Sinclair." In *After the Genteel Tradition*, Malcolm Cowley, ed. Carbondale: Southern Illinois, 1964.

Chalmers, David Mark. *The Social and Political Ideas of the Muckrakers.* New York: Citadel, 1964.

Dawson, Hugh J. "Winston Churchill and Upton Sinclair: An Early Review of *The Jungle.*" *American Literary Realism* 24 (1991): pp. 72–78.

DeGruson, Gene. "Introduction." In *The Lost First Edition of Upton Sinclair's* The Jungle. Atlanta: Peachtree Publishers, 1988.

Dell, Floyd. *Upton Sinclair: A Study in Social Protest.* New York: George H. Doran, 1960.

Dembo, L. S. *Detotalized Totalities: Synthesis and Disintegration in Naturalist, Existential, and Socialist Fiction.* Madison: University of Wisconsin Press, 1989.

———. "The Socialist and Socialite Heroes of Upton Sinclair." In *Toward a New American Literary History: Essays in Honor of Arlin Turner*, eds. Louis J. Budd, Edwin H. Cady, and Carl L. Anderson. Durham, North Carolina: Duke University Press, 1980.

Duram, James C. *Upton Sinclair's Realistic Romanticism.* Wichita, Kansas: Wichita State University, 1970.

French, Warren. *The Social Novel at the End of an Era.* Carbondale: Southern Illinois University, 1966.

Gilbert, James Burkhart. *Writers and Partisans: A History of Literary Radicalism in America*. New York: John Wiley and Sons, 1968.

Gilenson, Boris. "A Socialist of the Emotions: Upton Sinclair." *Twentieth Century American Literature: A Soviet View*, tr. by Ronald Vroon. Moscow: Progress Publishers, 1976.

Gonzalez Diaz, Isabel. "Whose Chicago, Anyway?: 'Aesthetics' vs. 'Propaganda' in Upton Sinclair's Ending for *The Jungle*." *Revista Canaria de Estudios Ingleses* 32–33 (April–November 1996): pp. 93–106.

Gottesman, Ronald. *A Catalogue of Books, Manuscripts, and Other Materials from the Upton Sinclair Archives*. Bloomington, Indiana: Lilly Library, 1963.

———, and Charles L. P. Silet. *The Literary Manuscripts of Upton Sinclair*. Columbus: Ohio State University, 1972.

———. *Upton Sinclair: An Annotated Checklist*. Kent, Ohio: Kent State University Press, 1973.

———. "The Upton Sinclair Dime Novels," *Dime Novel Round-up* 33 (March 15, 1964): pp. 20–23.

Grenier, Judson A. "Muckraking the Muckrakers: Upton Sinclair and His Peers." *In Reform and Reformers in the Progressive Era*, eds. David R. Colburn and George E. Pozzetta. Westport, Connecticut: Greenwood Press, 1983, pp. 71–92.

Grove, Dorys Crow. "Upton Sinclair: Never Forgotten." *Midamerica* 22 (1995): pp. 41–49.

Harris, Leon. *Upton Sinclair: American Rebel*. New York: Thomas Y. Crowell, 1975.

Herms, Dieter. "From West Point Cadet to Presidential Agent: Popular Literature Elements in Upton Sinclair." *The Upton Sinclair Quarterly* IV (December 1980): pp. 13–19.

———, ed. *Upton Sinclair: Literature and Social Reform*. Frankfurt: Peter Lang, 1990.

Herreshoff, David. "Upton Sinclair's *The Jungle*." *The American Socialist* III (November 1956): pp. 16–19.

Homberger, Eric. *American Writers and Radical Politics, 1900–39*. New York: St. Martin's Press, 1986.

Howard, June. *Form and History in American Literary Naturalism*. Chapel Hill and London: University of North Carolina Press, 1985.

Kazin, Alfred. *On Native Grounds*. New York: Doubleday, 1955.

Koerner, J. D. "The Last of the Muckrake Men." *South Atlantic Quarterly* 55 (April 1956): pp. 221–232.

Libman, Valentin A., comp.; Robert V. Allen, trans.; and Clarence Gohdes, ed. *Russian Studies of American Literature*. Chapel Hill, North Carolina: University of North Carolina Press, 1969.

Mencken, H. L. "A Moral Tale." *Nation* 133 (September 23, 1931): p. 310.

Morgan, H. Wayne. *American Socialism, 1900–1960*. Englewood Cliffs, New Jersey: Prentice Hall, 1964.

Parmentor, William. "*The Jungle* and Its Effects." *Journalism History* 10 (Spring–Summer 1983): pp. 14–15.

Rajanan, Busnagi. "Upton Sinclair's *The Jungle* Revisited." Indian Journal of American Studies XII (July 1982): pp. 49–54.

Rideout, Walter B. *The Radical Novel in the United States, 1900–1954*. Cambridge: Harvard University Press, 1956.

Scriabine, Christine. "The Writing of *The Jungle*," *Chicago History* 10 (Spring 1981): pp. 27–37.

Seltzer, Mark. "The Naturalist Machine." In *Bodies and Machines*. New York: Rutledge, 1992, pp. 25–44.

Sinclair, Upton. *The Autobiography of Upton Sinclair*, New York: Harcourt Brace, and
       World, 1962.
——. "Is 'The Jungle' True?," *Independent* 40 (May 17, 1906): pp. 1129–33.
Smith, C. S. "Upton Sinclair's *The Jungle*." *Chicago and the American Literary Imagi-
       nation*. Chicago: University of Chicago Press, 1984.
Suh, Suk Bong. "Lithuanian Wedding Traditions in Upton Sinclair's *The Jungle*."
       Lituanus: Baltic States Quarterly of Arts and Sciences 33, no. 1 (Winter 1987):
       pp. 5–17.
Swados, Harvey. "The World of Upton Sinclair." *Atlantic Monthly* (December 1961):
       pp. 96–102.
Tebbetts, Terrell, L. "Jurgis's Freedom: *The Jungle* as a Case for Familial Society."
       Lamar Journal of the Humanities 4, no. 2 (1978): pp. 15–20.
Wade, Louise Carroll. "The Problem with Classroom Use of Upton Sinclair's *The
       Jungle*." *American Studies* 32, no. 2 (1991): pp. 79–101.
Wilson, Christopher. "Upton Sinclair." In *The Labor of Words: Literary Professionalism
       in the Progressive Era*. Athens: University of Georgia Press, 1985.

Acknowledgments

"The Muckraker" by Jon A. Yoder. From *Upton Sinclair* by Jon A. Yoder. ©1975 by Frederick Ungar Publishing Co. Reprinted by permission.

"Upton Sinclair's Escape from *The Jungle:* The Narrative Strategy and Suppressed Conclusion of America's First Proletarian Novel" by Michael Brewster Folsom. From *Prospects: An Annual of American Cultural Studies.* ©1979 by Burt Franklin & Co., Inc. and Jack Salzman. Reprinted by permission.

"Introduction to *The Jungle*" by Morris Dickstein. From *The Jungle* by Upton Sinclair. Introduction ©1987 by Bantam Books, a division of Random House, Inc. Reprinted by permission.

"Upton Sinclair's *The Jungle* and Orwell's *Animal Farm:* A Relationship Explored" by Timothy Cook. From *Modern Fiction Studies* 30, no. 4 (Winter 1984): 696–702. ©1984 by Purdue Research Foundation. Reprinted by permission.

"Muckraking and Fame: *The Jungle*" by R. N. Mookerjee. From *Art for Social Justice: The Major Novels of Upton Sinclair* by R. N. Mookerjee. © 1988 by Scarecrow Press, Inc. Reprinted by permission.

"Afterword to *The Jungle*" by Emory Elliott. From *The Jungle* by Upton Sinclair. Afterword © 1990 by Emory Elliott. Reprinted by permission.

"*The Call of the Wild* and *The Jungle:* Jack London's and Upton Sinclair's Animal and Human Jungles" by Jacqueline Tavernier-Courbin. From *The Cambridge Companion to American Realism and Naturalism*, edited by Donald Pizer. © 1995 by Cambridge University Press. Reprinted by permission.

"What a Beating Feels Like: Authorship, Dissolution and Masculinity in Sinclair's *The Jungle*" by Scott Derrick. From *Studies in American Fiction* 23, no. 1 (Spring 1995): 85–100. © 1995 by Northeastern University. Reprinted by permission.

"The Two Lives of Jurgis Rudkus" by Matthew J. Morris. From *American Literary Realism: 1870–1910* 29, no. 2 (Winter 1997): 50–67. ©1997 by McFarland & Company, Inc. Reprinted by permission.

Index